MY FATHER AT 100

This Large Print Book carries the
Seal of Approval of N.A.V.H.

MY FATHER AT 100

RON REAGAN

THORNDIKE PRESS
A part of Gale, Cengage Learning

GALE
CENGAGE Learning

Detroit • New York • San Francisco • New Haven, Conn • Waterville, Maine • London

LIBRARY OF CONGRESS CATALOGING-IN-PUBLICATION DATA

Reagan, Ron, 1958–
   My father at 100 / by Ron Reagan.
     p. cm. — (Thorndike Press large print biography)
   Originally published: New York : Viking, 2011.
   ISBN-13: 978-1-4104-3437-1 (hardcover)
   ISBN-10: 1-4104-3437-0 (hardcover)
   1. Reagan, Ronald. 2. Reagan, Ronald — Family. 3. Presidents
— United States — Biography. I. Title. II. Title: My father at one
hundred.
   E877.R325 2011b
   973.927092—dc22
   [B]
                              2010051725

Published in 2011 by arrangement with Viking, a member of Penguin Group (USA) Inc.

Printed in Mexico
2 3 4 5 6 7 15 14 13 12 11

*To all the family members
whose stories I never knew
and
To Doria,
whose story is forever intertwined
with my own.*

ACKNOWLEDGMENTS

As a first-time author, I would have floundered without the help of many generous souls. I owe Clare Ferraro a debt of gratitude for taking a chance on me in the first place. Editor Rick Kot provided invaluable advice; his thoughtfulness and thoroughness are matched only by his deft, light touch. Thanks also to Laura Tisdel, Kyle Davis, Rachel Burd, Francesca Belanger, and Gregg Kulick. No book would have been possible without the hard work of Laurie Jacoby, a friend and ally for many years, and Lydia Wills. I'm profoundly grateful to both. There were helping hands all along the way. At the Reagan Presidential Library my job was made considerably easier by Mike Duggan, Steve Branch, Kirby Elizabeth Hanson, Joanne Drake, and Wren Powell. In Tampico, Illinois, I received invaluable help from Joan Johnson along with David and Judy Jacobson. In Dixon, I was warmly received and aided by Connie Lange, Sue Little, Phyllis Scherer, Arlene Waterhouse, Marla Tremble, and William Jones. Eureka College also rolled out the welcome mat. Special thanks to Eureka's president, Dr. J. David Arnold, Brian Sjalko, Anthony Glass, and Jyl Krause. Jim Santanella provided invaluable technical help. Deepest thanks as well to my mother, Nancy Reagan, for her enthusiastic support every step of the way and to my wife, Doria, for her love and patience.

CONTENTS

INTRODUCTION

Through the sepia of the old photograph, I can make out the man, his left foot casually crossed over the right, leaning against the corner post of a storefront window display. He has removed his jacket, keeping buttoned a vest of dark wool that matches his neatly pressed trousers. With his arms folded, his white shirtsleeves cross his chest, revealing stiffly starched cuffs fastened by cuff links. A bright white collar with a dark necktie snugly knotted beneath sets off a noticeably bronzed complexion, but the features of his face, awash in morning sunlight, are hard to make out beyond a thick flop of hair over the left brow and a pair of noticeably prominent ears. Above him, a sign announces: CLOTH-ING SALE. I read the handwritten inscription on the picture's lower border: *Suppose you know the fellow in his shirtsleeves . . .*

It takes me a moment to put things together, but then I suppose I do. The man in the doorway of the H. C. Pitney Variety Store in Tampico, Illinois, is my grandfather, John Edward ("Jack") Reagan. The photograph appears to have been taken between 1906 and 1914, right around the time of my father's birth, which would put Jack in his mid- to late twenties. The inscription, written years later by his wife, Nelle, my grandmother, was most likely intended for one of her two sons, John Neil (Moon) or Ronald. This is the first time I've laid eyes on it.

I'm sitting in the research room of the Ronald Reagan Presidential Foundation and Library in Simi Valley, California, some 1,600 miles and roughly a century removed from that sunny morning in Tampico, feeling a bit like an archaeologist sifting through the scant relics of my family's ancient past. Actually, I'm feeling like a very fortunate and pampered archaeologist. Many folks these days are exploring their family histories; not many have an entire research facility eagerly helping with the effort. A Spanish-style edifice of ochre stucco commanding a rolling ridge of grass and chaparral north of Los Angeles, the Reagan Library holds, as you would expect, a vast trove of presidential papers as well as documents from my father's days as governor. But it has also become a repository for various and sundry items connected to my family, including the kind of personal artifacts that have a way of turning up in the bottoms of trunks or slipping from between the pages of family Bibles.

Where, I wonder, did this photo and several others like it come from? Mike Duggan, the library's supervisory archivist, can't say. He carefully removes several musty Dixon High School yearbooks from their tissue paper wrappings, cautions me to handle them using the white cotton gloves he has provided, and heads off to check with Steve Branch, who is in charge of audiovisual material. Steve, it turns out, believes the pictures must have been sent over by my mother after one of her periodic housecleaning campaigns. When I check with her later that night, however, she pleads ignorance. From my description of the photos, she doesn't believe she's familiar with them. I'm left wondering whether my father — so reflexively guarded in his privacy — for some mysterious reason kept hidden from his loved ones a small treasury of family photos, including many of his own father as a young man and some of the only pictures I've ever seen of his aunts and uncles. "That would be odd," my mother agrees. *Yes,* I think to myself, *but not altogether surprising.*

Setting my suspicions aside — it's conceivable the photos were donated to the library by Dad's brother, Moon, I focus back on the photograph itself. It and a similarly captioned companion are the clearest look I've had at the world into which my father was born. Tampico, his original hometown — then and now a postage stamp on a flat patch of farmland in north central Illinois, a little over 100 miles west of Chicago — looks a bare half step evolved from Dodge City. None of the brick or clapboard storefronts stands more than two stories. The sidewalks are raised above a dirt thoroughfare, the better to keep mud and worse from being flung at pedestrians by the wheels of passing carts and carriages. There are hitching posts where parking meters might be today. Only the electrical wires strung overhead hint at modernity.

The other photo provides a view across the street, with the apartment where the Reagan family lived at the time identified by an X etched in ink. Another, ruder X next door has been rubbed out. *Jack had the wrong flat marked so I put the cross on the right one,* my grandmother has written below.

The photographer's own caption says, "Busy Day, Main Street," which appears to be no exaggeration. Outside, in the street below the flat, I count 20 horse-drawn conveyances of various descriptions, from farm wagons to sport buggies. The sidewalks are lively, mostly with men, who stand talking in small clusters in front of the post office and J. R. Howlett's hardware store. Charles Darby's tailor shop — CLEANING AND REPAIRING A SPECIALTY — graciously offers those who care to linger a LUNCH ROOM. And there, in the middle of the block, its new awning capturing the photographer's attention as it would that of any potential customer, sits H. C. Pitney's competition: JOHN BACKLUND HAS TURNED THE BIG GUNS LOOSE, promises (threatens?) an enormous sign hung across the front of the building. Below the lettering a caricature of a man wearing a derby and an aggressive mustache — perhaps John Backlund himself — fires a cannon at a disreputable lout representing "High Prices." EVERY CENT COUNTS HERE, banners proclaim. BIG VALUES IN MEN'S SUITS. OPPORTUNITY KNOCKS TODAY. Another, centrally positioned, reminds shoppers, WE MUST HAVE CASH. John Backlund isn't the sort of merchant who tolerates bumpkins showing up hoping to purchase a new Sunday suit with a basket of eggs. I can imagine Jack Reagan standing in the doorway of the Pitney Store

15

across the street — judging by the angle, he could be looking over the photographer's shoulder — and casting a worried eye up at his own little sign.

Referring to the view of their old apartment, Nelle has written, *Just imagine that you see me with my head stuck out the window.* I peer at the fragile photograph in its plastic sleeve and do my best to comply. Casting my mind back across the years, I search for a glimpse of auburn hair radiant in the falling light of a lingering summer evening as my young grandmother leans out over her windowsill, hoping to catch sight of her Jack as he comes whistling his way home from another day selling shoes.

These scenes from a century past are at once familiar — the Pitney Store is long gone, but the building that housed it still stands — and alien. There is no mistaking it: This is a different world, one that existed a very long time ago. At the same time, it is maddeningly near — as close as a single generation. My father was born in that very flat overlooking that same busy street filled with the comings and goings of farmers and their teams of horses. Though my grandfather, Jack, was killed by a heart attack 17 years before I was born, the woman leaning out of that window lived long enough to know

16

me in my infancy. All at once, the reality of my father's age, the gulf separating his early, small-town life in the farm country of Illinois — its rustling leaves, jingling bridles, and barnyard smells — from the hypercosmopolitan, pop culture–obsessed, global-tweeting maelstrom that is modern America comes crashing home.

My father would be 100 years old by now? There's something slightly unreal about that. Is it really possible? People whose parents have reached the century mark themselves usually seem to be in their seventies or at least late sixties. Not me. At 52 , I'm not even close to eligibility for the benefits of socialized medicine. I still have all my teeth and hair (though an increasing amount of gray appears to be creeping into the latter, and my dentist has, of late, been shooting me dirty looks). Yet here I am, faced with the astounding yet unavoidable truth: My very own father was born in 1911, and that is, yes, 100 years ago.

Admittedly, he didn't actually make it all the way himself, dying after a long, lingering swoon into the abyss of dementia in 2004, at the age of 93. But he came respectably close nonetheless. Close enough, I say. We won't quibble over those few years he fell short — not least because, with his name still on so many lips, he seems so strangely present even now.

His was a life that spanned the twentieth century, stopping along the way in venues as quintessentially American as the small-town Midwest, Golden Age Hollywood, and 1600 Pennsylvania Avenue. A little boy who chased after horse-drawn ice wagons grew up to act in movies alongside the likes of Bette Davis and Errol Flynn and grew old as the leader of the free world, responsible for the planet's most powerful nuclear arsenal. He lived through perhaps the most astonishing period of change — material, technological, cultural — that our nation has known. He witnessed virtually the whole progression, finding it alternately inspiring, horrific, and utterly baffling. His life's journey marked him, shaped him, as it would anyone. But the approach, perspective, and character he brought to it had their roots in a world that no longer exists. Ronald Reagan, who was the most dynamic American political figure of the late twentieth century, whose name remains at the center of policy debates to this day, was an emissary from our nation's past.

"What are you going to tell me about him that I don't already know?" This question from an old friend when told I was writing

18

this book is entirely legitimate if a bit disquieting. One of the difficulties in even contemplating an account of my father's life comes with realizing that everyone thinks he's long since learned anything worth knowing about Ronald Reagan — film actor, governor of California, and, most especially, president of the United States. He is among the most scrutinized, analyzed, chronicled, and pondered figures of our time, with oceans of ink and broad swaths of forest having been sacrificed to the effort. Reporters, historians, former associates, biographers official and unofficial — all have weighed in, rendering their various judgments positive, negative, and just plain confounded. Journalists such as Lou Cannon — a Reagan watcher since the California governorship — have devoted the better part of their careers to tracing his political trajectory. Estimable observers such as Garry Wills and Richard Reeves, among others, have weighed in. Pulitzer Prize–winning biographer Edmund Morris — to whom I'm greatly indebted for his prodigious research — spent years tailing Dad as his Boswell, producing the searching and deeply felt but much misunderstood *Dutch: A Memoir of Ronald Reagan,* which in fact comes as near as any book I've read to capturing my father's elusive nature. Martin

Anderson, a former economic and policy adviser to my father, along with his wife, Annelise, have put together several collections of his speeches, diaries, letters, and other writings — an invaluable compendium of original material. Adding to the library, Dad published two autobiographies: *Where's the Rest of Me?* came out during his initial run for governor of California in 1965; *An American Life* was released in 1990, after he had left the presidency. My mother and siblings, too, have all written at least one book, each extensively chronicling their experiences with our famous family member.

Since his death, my father has also been incessantly trotted out as a totem for various (mostly right-wing) causes, not all of which he would support. While he remains a bête noire to many on the left, some progressives have come to reconsider him more charitably, particularly in light of the most recent Republican administration. It all stacks up to a lot of research, verbiage, and consideration devoted to my father, so a certain skepticism regarding what his youngest son could possibly add to the record is understandable.

But the question also embraces a faulty premise. You may think you know Ronald Reagan, or at least the 90 percent or so that was so long and frequently on public display. Who wouldn't recognize the trademark wink and nod, the thick, seemingly invincible head of hair, the soft burr of his voice? A husky "Well . . ." with a tip of the head is all a comedian or mimic needs to offer for an audience to know immediately who is being impersonated. Most people will be acquainted, too, with the rudiments of his life story: birth in a little Illinois farm town; pious mother; hard-drinking father; radio sports announcer; middling movie star; wildly successful politician; leader of the free world. More than most celebrated figures, he obliterated the distinction between public and private personas. The Ronald Reagan people watched for decades, particularly as a politician — giving speeches, meeting other world leaders, reacting to events joyous or calamitous — was essentially the same man his family saw around the dinner table. Did he seem buoyant and even-tempered? True enough. Dignified and resolute? No argument there. Stubborn and resistant to evidence that confounded his predilections? That, too. However, even to those of us who were closest to him, that hidden 10 percent remains a considerable mystery.

His children, if they were being honest, would agree that he was as strange a fellow as any of us had ever met. Not darkly strange, mind you. In fact, he was so naturally sunny, so utterly without guile, so devoid of cynicism or pettiness as to create for himself a whole new category of strangeness. He was, in some respects, too good — like a visitor from an enchanted realm where they'd never even consider inventing a Double Down sandwich or credit default swaps. I often felt I had to check my natural sarcasm and sense of absurdity at the door for fear of inducing in him a fit of psychological disequilibrium. In his presence, profanity often felt out of place. Not that he was prudishly above a "smoking car story," as he would put it with a charming if slightly bizarre anachronism, but only after any women within a half-mile radius had been safely sequestered in a soundproof booth.

Unlike my siblings — taking their memoirs at face value — I never felt particularly deprived of my father's company. This was partly due to circumstance. I am the younger of two children from his second (final) marriage to Nancy Davis. My elder sister, Maureen, and brother, Mike, spent much of the time with their own mother, Jane Wyman, his first wife, and only occasionally visited their father and his new family. Intrafamilial tensions and estrangements were a predictable result. In the meantime, there was only one set of parents for me to worry about. My sister, Patti, shares that advantage, but being six years older than me, was off to boarding school by the time I reached the age of seven or eight. I ended up being raised, during the school year at least, virtually as an only child, with no shortage of attention coming my way, for better or worse. Particularly when I was a small boy and his television work permitted him sufficient free time, Dad was one of my favorite — and most reliable — playmates. My mother might shoo me away — "Daddy's got work to do" — but I could almost always count on coaxing him out from behind his desk for a swim or a game of catch. I had him pegged early on as essentially an overgrown kid.

As I grew older, though, I began to recognize the qualities in our father that my brother and sisters experienced as distant and inattentive. He was often wandering somewhere in his own head. I never felt that he didn't love or care for me, but occasionally he seemed to need reminding about basic aspects of my life — like birthdays, who my friends were, or how I was doing in school. I could share an hour of warm camaraderie with Dad, then once I'd walked out the door, get the uncanny feeling I'd disappeared into the wings of his mind's stage, like a character no longer necessary to the ongoing story line.

A paradoxical character, my father: He was warm yet remote. As affable as they come, he had, in his later life, virtually no close friends besides his wife. He thrived on public display, yet remained intensely private. Forceful in the role of political leader, he was, in person, surprisingly soft-spoken and gentle. More than willing to call Soviet leaders to account, fully capable of snatching up the microphone at a presidential primary debate and backhanding the moderator — "I'm paying for this microphone, Mr. Green!" — behind the scenes he shied away from conflict. Tenderhearted and sentimental in his personal dealings, he could nevertheless have difficulty extending his sympathies to abstract classes of people, an obliviousness that was, understandably, taken for callousness.

Even his movie career revealed contradictions. While he was an astonishingly good-looking, extremely photogenic man — I'll bet even the shot on his driver's license was a keeper — he, nevertheless, generally failed to project onscreen the urgent sexuality, the heat, that made some of his contemporaries like Flynn, Clark Gable, even Humphrey

Bogart genuine movie stars.

The preeminent American leader of the late twentieth century, whose voice still resonates in the twenty-first, he remained to the end of his days, in many respects, a child of the nineteenth. "You know," he once told me, "I don't feel any different inside now than I did when I was young." I never doubted it.

The occasional Father's Day remembrance aside, I have long resisted writing about Dad's life or offering a memoir of our lives together. Doing so while he held office always struck me as exploitive, not to mention unfair to a loved one in such a vulnerable position. Then, too, it posed all the difficulties of painting a portrait while literally nose to nose with your subject. His fundamental inscrutability notwithstanding, we were quite close as father and son, so I can't exactly claim to have a dispassionate, removed perspective. Beyond that, undertaking a study of his past just seemed odd like rifling his drawers while he was out to dinner. So why do it now?

It was the century anniversary that changed my mind. I had been talking to my mother on the occasion of Dad's ninety-ninth birthday. She steered the conversation toward the planned centennial celebrations. "Can you

believe Daddy would have been a hundred?"
(She still calls him Daddy to her kids, Ronnie
to their friends.) I responded warmly along
the lines of, "Wow, yeah . . . really amaz-
ing . . . hard to believe" — though without
a level of excitement suggesting any eagerness to attend the unveiling of another new
Ronald Reagan bridge. I'm sure my mother
would welcome my involvement in more official Reagan commemorations, but I prefer
to recall him without the aid of eponymous
aircraft carriers and interstate highways.

Later that night, though, and in the days
that followed, I couldn't get the thought out
of my head. *A hundred years*. Such a long
time past; so much history made in the meantime; so many changes taken place since his
birth. What was it like to be a youngster so
long ago, growing up in a world without cell
phones, television, or, for a time, even radio?
How did it feel to be awakened mornings by
the sound of horses stamping their hooves in
the street below?

Well aware of how I've been influenced by
my Cold War, heavy-metal, sexual revolu-
tion youth, I wondered how he was molded
by his own experiences in a radically different America of haystacks, flappers, bathtub
gin, and the Great Depression. All of us are
time travelers, lugging into the future our

baggage from the past. What was my father carrying with him from a century ago?

Over the years I missed many opportunities to question my father directly about his early life. Though I have long been interested in our family's genealogy, as a child and younger man I never thought to press him much about his close relatives or the details of his growing up. In his later years Alzheimer's disease robbed us of those moments. To be honest, though, he didn't exactly welcome that kind of interrogation. Spontaneous and novel reminiscenses about his past were relatively few and far between. He relied, instead, on a standard repertoire of stories, any of which could be promptly rolled forth onto his conversational rails as the situation warranted or allowed. Chatting with him over dinner, for instance, I might suddenly become aware that something I'd said, some trigger word inadvertently deployed, had set his wheels in motion. A story was already emerging from the train shed and, now, anything I had to say, any possible point I might have hoped to make, was rendered irrelevant. He would begin by looking at me eagerly, with just a touch of impatience, and I'd realize he was only waiting for me to pause for breath so he could switch tracks. "Have I ever told you about the time . . . ?" Resistance was futile. On the only occasion I recall pointedly telling him that we'd all heard that story plenty of times before, he looked so crestfallen that I silently pledged never again to inflict that kind of pain on any living creature.

All of his stories — including, no doubt, some he didn't share — add up to *the* story: the relentlessly rolling saga of Ronald Reagan, as imagined, rehearsed, and recounted from his earliest boyhood onward, by him.

We all cobble together an internal account of our lives; in that, Dad was entirely typical. Virtually everyone creates a mental album of memories and anecdotes that, ultimately, passes for our version of a life story. We are all the protagonists of our own narratives, of course — the indispensable main character; on a good day, the hero. In that sense, Dad was just like everyone else. Only peculiarly more so. For most of us, the boundaries of our personal tale are relatively fluid and amenable to outside influence. Our story selection, even the sense of our own character, shifts as new circumstances arise: One day we're a rebel folk hero in the making, the next day, a contented corporate cog. But Dad's story, I believe, was far more comprehensive in its sweep and consistent in its

28

narrative details than is the case for most people. Keeping its primary themes intact and inviolate, safe from the depredations of an intrusive, ambiguous, and contradictory world, was for him an endeavor of existential import. My father didn't create his personal narrative to put one over on anyone. On the contrary, with its creation, he was forming a template for his life. He wanted to be seen — he wanted to truly be — an estimable individual who made his way through life as a positive force in the world, a man people would admire for all the right reasons.

Critics have long accused him of falseness, of merely acting out assigned roles. Such a superficial analysis ignores the central curiosity of my father's character: He played only one role, ever, and he did so unconsciously, totally absorbed in its performance.

Reading his early high school and college essays, and considering his film career, among other things — and with plenty of opportunity for personal observation along the way — I see two primary threads jumping out of my father's story line: that fierce desire to be recognized as someone noteworthy, even heroic; and his essentially solitary nature.

On the one hand, he reveled in public exposure — the bigger the stage, the more comfortable he was. He warmed to applause and the approval of crowds. He counted on the support of those around him. But in the film unwinding in his mind, Dad was always the loner, compassionate yet detached, who rides to the rescue in reel three. This role could become tedious — it's fun to be bad on occasion — and would prove unhelpful to his professional goals, for just as Hollywood was marketing ambivalent antiheroes, Dad was looking to wear an unblemished white hat in conventional westerns. Yet when he became a politician, circumstance and story line meshed beautifully: Don't we want our presidents to be heroes?

Ronald Reagan was the inverse of an iceberg: Most of him — the public man — was plainly visible above the surface. Public Reagan sought glory on his college football team and when he broadcast sports events over the radio, acted in films, and entered the political arena with great success. He wanted and needed acclaim and recognition. At the same time, he would disavow ambition: It was crucial to his sense of self that he be seen working on behalf of others, and not for personal gain. But all the while, another, quieter Reagan, just as vital, rested invisibly beneath the waves. This hermetic self, who found outward expression mostly in the solitary acts of writing, ranch work, and swimming, was, in effect, the producer and director for the man onstage. In this Private Reagan, the personal drive he publicly forswore burned with a cold but steady flame. This private self, glimpsed only in fleeting, unguarded moments, formed his core. Without public acclaim, he may have been unfulfilled. Deprived of the opportunity to take refuge in his castle of solitude, he would have withered altogether. The Ronald Reagan with whom everyone is familiar could not have existed without the Ronald Reagan he rarely let anyone see.

The roots of that bicameral character and the foundation of his story's arc must be traced back to his early life — a life beginning in a distant, early twentieth-century America, an America quite different from the country we inhabit today. Without some understanding of that story and the role he fashioned for himself within it, there is no real reckoning with Ronald Reagan.

This is not a political biography — that's a job best left for others. I argued plenty with my father while he was alive; I have no intention of picking a fight with him now that he's gone and can't defend himself. Neither does this book pretend to be an encyclopedic recounting of his entire life. It is simply my attempt to come to grips with the father with whom I grew up, with a public figure both revered and reviled and, most important, with a human being in all his stubborn enigma. Everyone thinks he knows Ronald Reagan, but those who truly knew him best still grapple with the enduring mystery of his inner character. I'm hoping that some light might penetrate that mystery if I can focus on the man I knew through the lens of his early, formative years.

What follows, then, is a layer cake of stories: A running account of my search through my father's early life (with some admittedly amateurish general history thrown in for context); a memoir of our lives together as father and son; and, finally, an exploration of his personal, internal narrative — the story of his story, a tale already germinating a century ago.

But my storytelling father came from somewhere. His family had a history, as well. So let's begin even further back in time, across the Atlantic, some hundred years earlier still, before the storyteller himself enters the picture.

CHAPTER ONE
THE O'REGANS OF DOOLIS

Turns out we're related to every royal family in Europe . . . [pause for effect] . . . except King Zog of Albania." My father's inflection and timing seemed to suggest that if you were forced to toss overboard just one royal household on the continent, Zog's would be the one to get the heave-ho. The British monarchy: Now *that* was a royal family worth claiming relation to. France had its Louis — tragic yet high profile. But Zog? No offense to the Albanian people, mind you, fiercely proud as they must be, but claiming connection to every other royal except Albania's peculiarly named king frankly made for a better story. The Zog business provided a welcome punch line, defusing what might otherwise be taken for a boast.

Things change when you are elected president of the United States. In 1981, when my father moved into the White House, having routed his predecessor, Jimmy Carter, by a wider than expected margin in the previous year's election, he traded substantial celebrity for incandescent world renown. Daily life took on a very different cast. The commute to work couldn't have been much shorter, but, if long-distance travel was required, he now had his own plane fueled up and ready to go. A helicopter, too. Or, if he preferred, a custom-designed armored limousine was on hand to whisk him anywhere his heart desired.

Presidents travel in style. The trappings of fame can be taken for granted. Appearances on the front pages of national newspapers and periodicals become routine. Heads of state drop in to visit. Brass bands have a habit of striking up whenever you walk into a room. And people seemed eager to do things for you — like trace your family history.

So it was that we came to learn of our rather tenuous connection to royalty. A company specializing in genealogical research, Burke's Peerage, in celebration of my father's visit to his ancestral Irish homeland, provided us with our personal family tree. Looking it over, I couldn't help but notice that, despite our ostensible royal relatives, the tree was conspicuously lacking in visible crowned heads of state. Apparently there was not enough paper available to adequately convey the distance between the bog Irish O'Regans of Tipperary and the Windsors of Buckingham Palace. We may have been related to royalty, but in such a twelfth-cousin-million-times-removed kind of way that we'd certainly be ushered to the servant's entrance should we ever have a mind to drop by for a visit at any "ancestral" estate.

I'm fairly certain that in their eagerness to flatter, the genealogists had neglected to mention that virtually everyone of European descent can claim some distant relation to members of most, if not all, royal European households (Zog's being a possible exception). The exponential addition of progenitors as we travel back generation by generation virtually guarantees this. We all have 2 parents, 4 grandparents, 8 great-grandparents, and so forth. By the time we reach 20 generations — about the year 1500, give or take — we have reached 1,048,578 18X great-grandparents; at thirty generations — roughly the thirteenth century — our ancestors would, theoretically, number over a billion. That's more people than the entire population of the planet during that period. Is it any wonder we're all related — paupers, shopkeepers, and kings? Being linked to royalty has an obvious appeal for many, but it is equally true that we are all connected to just about every highwayman, scullery maid, and plague carrier as well. Just as with every breath we inhale oxygen molecules breathed by the Buddha and by Hitler, so we may claim kinship with Marie Antoinette, but we are just as likely to be a distant cousin to Madame Defarge (figuratively speaking). No matter, Dad, who never lost sight of his modest midwestern upbringing, was clearly enthralled by the notion of our blue-blood connections, however remote.

We had both been pleased to discover — some 12 years earlier, when my father was governor of California — that the name Reagan was said to derive from a nephew of the great tenth-century Irish warrior king Brian Boru, a red-bearded, sword-wielding, Dark Ages hero with sure-fire appeal for young boys and their whimsical fathers. For years Boru kept himself busy questing after the high kingship of Ireland, marrying various wives, siring sundry offspring, hectoring the island's dominant O'Neal family, and harassing the Norse invaders who controlled Dublin. On April 23, 1014, having reached what was, under the circumstances, a shockingly ripe old age of 73, he met his bloody end at the Battle of Clontarf. Somewhere amid all that hacking, plundering, and procreating, a brother of Boru apparently decided to call one of his own sons Reagan, a name that in those days sported an extra vowel or two and is thought to have been pronounced something like Ree-gawn. Thus the Reagan family line was born — or so the story goes. (Political historians take note: Boru's full name was Brian Bóruma mac Cennótig, making us distant relations of the Kennedy clan as well.)

Relatives in chain mail and armor were all well and good, but by the time I reached my twenties, I couldn't help being drawn to the other, more plausible names on our family tree — names in which, I couldn't help but notice, my father seemed curiously uninterested. Whether this was because Burke's had focused almost exclusively on his father's forebears and some residual scorn for wayward Jack extended to his kin, or because he found impoverished, hard-drinking farm laborers of little interest I don't know, but Dad hardly gave his actual ancestors — as opposed to the theoretical ennobled variety — a second glance. Undeterred and armed with this newly minted family tree, a handful of names, and a fascination with them I couldn't quite explain, I became our family's default genealogist.

A soft wind blowing sweet and warm
From the peaks called Knockmeal Down . . .

There is some uncertainty as to the date and place of birth of Thomas O'Regan, the earliest certain ancestor bearing my father's family name; 1783 is the year most frequently mentioned. But did Thomas first draw breath in the shadow of Knockmealdown Peak on the border of counties Tipperary and Waterford in southern Ireland, or a few miles to the north, somewhere on the flanks of the more imposing Galtee Mountains? Available records confusingly mention both locations. Whichever peat and heather–covered high ground he called home — and soft Irish breezes notwithstanding — he was, perhaps inevitably, born into one of Ireland's endlessly successive periods of strife.

Penal laws imposed by Britain in the early eighteenth century had, for decades, deprived Irish Catholics — who comprised approximately 90 percent of the island's population — of fundamental rights. They could not vote, hold office, own land, or possess a horse of any substantial value. They were deprived of opportunities for education. (The subsequent lack of records can create an often insurmountable barrier to tracing one's Irish roots.)

Absentee Anglo-Irish landlords, almost exclusively Protestant, siphoned off nearly a quarter of Ireland's GDP by the end of the century. They frequently rented out their lands to tenant farmers who, in turn, would allow poor laborers like Thomas O'Regan to build homes and keep small garden patches on the property in exchange for dawn-to-dusk work in the fields. Given the typical Irish temperament, these draconian restrictions and economic inequities were bound to meet resistance. By the middle of the 1700s, secret societies of Irish Catholics with names like the Whiteboys, the Rightboys, the Hearts of Oak, and the Steelboys had begun to agitate for redress. Landlord's barns were burned to the ground, their cattle hamstrung; shillelaghs swung from hedgerows bordering darkened lanes, cracking the skulls of English sympathizers. For a brief period, the British government relented, granting Ireland an independent parliament. The Insurrection of 1798, led by Wolfe Tone among others, put an end to such attempts at conciliation. Fighting, where it broke out, was savage and marked by mercilessness on both sides. Irish separatists armed with pikes and clubs ultimately squared off against British muskets and cannons at Vinegar Hill in County Wexford and were, in the words of one observer, cut down "like new mown grass."

As has often been the case in Ireland, tragic defeat was turned into a drinking song. "The Boys of Wexford" has rung out from Irish pubs ever since:

We are the boys of Wexford
Who fought with heart and hand.
To burst in twain the galling chain
And free our native land.

By 1801 the British had reasserted control with the Act of Union, formally annexing Ireland to the United Kingdom. Only in Ireland could such a century of turmoil be referred to as the Long Peace.

It is anyone's guess how Thomas O'Regan reacted to these events, but it's a near certainty that his mind was fixed primarily on survival. Living conditions for the typical Irish peasant were, by virtually any civilized standards, a shocking exercise in coarseness and deprivation. Although Tipperary was perhaps not the most impoverished county in all of Ireland, over a third of its population lived in what were regarded as "fourth-class" accommodations — in other words, abject squalor. Fewer than 1 in 10 could read or write. The typical lower-class home was a windowless hovel fashioned of wattle and daub (mud and sticks) with a central hearth that wafted blue peat smoke not up a chimney but through a hole in a perennially leaking roof. Additional heat was provided in winter by cattle and pigs invited to commingle in the tight confines of the dirt-floored dwelling. Furniture, such as it was, consisted of little more than a bed shared by all and, perhaps, a chair or bench. The vast majority of the rural poor would have lived out their lives never traveling more than a day's walk from their homes. News of the outer world would come rarely. Hunger, though, was a common visitor; disease ran unchecked. Life expectancy for the common Irish citizen of the time was low, barely 40 years at the beginning of the nineteenth century.

So it must have been for young Thomas O'Regan. By 1818 or so, he has moved from his mountainside home to the valley between the Galtees and Knockmealdowns. The much larger Golden Vale on the north side of the Galtees is paid more attention by visitors, but Thomas's new home boasts as exceptionally rich a soil as you'll find on the Emerald Isle, well watered by streams from the surrounding hills. There he marries a Tipperary girl, Margaret Murphy,

41

just half his age.

Today's accounts generally misplace their original O'Regan homestead in the town of Ballyporeen — a mistake the local burghers have been understandably reluctant to correct. With my father's rise to political prominence, Ballyporeen became the epicenter for everything Reagan-related in Ireland. They even renamed the pub after him, among the highest of honors bestowed in the land of Guinness.

In 1984, on his way to an economic summit in London, Dad literally helicoptered in to Ballyporeen. Though my parents and I had visited Ireland 15 years earlier, we had skipped our ostensible ancestral village. This, then, was Dad's first glimpse of the ground his forefathers had walked. He checked the parish register for his great-grandfather's name; he was led to the namesake pub where he dutifully hoisted a pint; he was introduced to a young man who looked shockingly like him — an experience he describes in his autobiography as "eerie." "Although I've never been a great one for introspection or dwelling on the past," he writes, with almost gymnastic understatement,

as I looked down the narrow main street of the little town from which an emigrant named Michael Reagan had set out in pursuit of a dream, I had a flood of thoughts, not only about Michael Reagan, but about his son, my grandfather whom I had never met. . . . What an incredible country we lived in, where the great-grandson of a poor immigrant from Ballyporeen could become president.

Well, yes, and if not you, then some other great-grandson of some other immigrant from somewhere else. That's the way America works. But what about that "flood of thoughts"? One can't expect a primarily political memoir to dwell too long on such matters, but I would, for years, fruitlessly try to arouse in him some genuine interest in his ancestry. A decade later, in 1994, when Dad was descending in the grip of Alzheimer's disease, I showed him a pencil-sketched family tree I had been working on. I watched as his eyes moved hazily over the page. "Hmmm . . . well . . . how about that?" he murmured. *I'm too late,* I thought.

The pub in Ballyporeen has since closed down, its owners selling its sign and many of its interior fittings to the Ronald Reagan Library. I guess the once-sustaining tourist trade dropped off when my father vacated the Oval Office. The local priest, though, will presumably still be happy to show interested visitors the old parish register containing the names of Thomas O'Regan; his wife, Margaret, and their children, most especially Michael.

Thomas and Margaret O'Regan appear to have had eight children between 1819 and 1829. There is some confusion around the first two, Nicholas and Ellen — both seem to have been born in the same year. Were Thomas and Margaret particularly fertile around this time or were Nicholas and Ellen actually twins? Evidence one way or the other is lacking. In any case, the pair was followed in 1821 by another brother, John, then by two sisters, Margaret and Elizabeth, in 1823 and 1826, and finally, in 1829, by their youngest son, Michael. The O'Regan home, local lore notwithstanding, was not in Ballyporeen but a few miles to the west in a collection of rude huts called Doolis. Sadly, there is no Doolis city council left to trumpet this news. Some years ago, on an ancestor-seeking foray to Tipperary, I discovered that Doolis had reverted to bog, its meager dwellings long since returned to the elements from which they were fashioned.

It is almost certain that neither Thomas nor Margaret could read or write. Most of their children would likely have fared no better in terms of formal education. The U.S. Census of 1860, which records eldest son Nicholas living in Fairhaven, Illinois, lists him as illiterate. But Michael was different. Somehow, somewhere — perhaps in one of the informal "hedge schools" that sprang up in defiance of British attempts to Anglicize the Irish citizenry — he acquired an at least rudimentary literacy. This in turn may have led to his becoming the first in his family's memory to make a living at something other than pulling potatoes out of the ground. Armed with the ability to scratch out and decipher markings on a page, young Michael O'Regan went to work at a soap factory in Ballyporeen — not a glamorous employ, but I suppose it's a notable step up from digging spuds.

The question of ambition — how powerful it was, and directed to what end — has been a persistent theme for biographers and historians intent on examining my father's life. If such a thing as a drive to exceed the expectations of one's station in life can be said to come down through the blood, then in Thomas O'Regan's youngest son we may be glimpsing its early stirrings.

Was he cocky, this Michael O'Regan? Arrogant and proud? Did he announce early on his intentions to rise beyond the bog and potato patch, to distinguish himself from his parents and siblings through sheer force of will? Or was he a quiet type, moving patiently, incrementally toward a dream he held close?

My father, coming from working-class circumstances far less deprived than those of his great-grandfather, nevertheless needed a scholarship worth half his tuition to become the first in his family to attend college. When asked on his junior year scholarship loan application what his plans were for a prospective career, Dad wrote, "I have no definite plans for the future outside of trying to get a position in some business probably as a salesman."

A salesman? Perhaps he had no definite plans, but Ronald Reagan had, by that time, begun dreaming in earnest of a future well beyond his father's shoe trade, one that would elevate him into the public eye. His boyhood fantasies of gridiron glory might have had to be shelved in deference to poor eyesight and less than blazing speed, but there was always acting, something for which he'd already developed an affinity, an enthusiasm he stoked with regular visits to local movie houses. Football hero; dashing celluloid star: My young father already wanted to be somebody, a figure to be respected and admired. Yet he was cautious, understandably so. In the Depression era Midwest, telling a loan officer you intended to ship off to Hollywood in hopes of becoming a movie star was roughly tantamount to announcing a desire to cross-dress at the next farm auction. But his caution, if that's what it was, ran deeper. During his entire time in movies and politics, my father would remain wary of being seen as a striver. As a politician, he would always have you believe that he was a reluctant candidate — he became a governor, then president, only because people insisted they needed him. It is one of the paradoxes of Dad's life that a powerful drive to court public acclaim by lifting himself to some heroic realm, mythic or real, was bound to an equally compelling need to keep that ambition under wraps.

Whether Michael O'Regan felt similarly compelled to disavow his desires is anyone's guess, but ambition was clearly part of his makeup. Of course, ambition sometimes needs a kick-start, and there's nothing quite like mortal peril to concentrate the mind.

If you had to choose just one food on which to subsist, you could do much worse than the humble potato. Rich in essentials like protein and carbohydrates, loaded with minerals and vitamin C, potatoes alone will keep a body alive, if not entirely satisfied, for the duration. Wheat, barley, and rice can't make the same claim. As a consequence, the overall health of potato-eating Irish peasants in Michael O'Regan's day was actually marginally better than that of their British brethren across the Irish Sea, who fared worse on a diet consisting primarily of bread. But English peasants had the advantage of variety. Wheat, barley, oats — if one crop failed due to inclement weather or blight, another could tide them over. In mid-nineteenth-century Ireland, though, there was, by British decree, virtually one crop only: a medium-sized white spud known as the Irish lumper. Behind every stone wall and hedgerow, in every garden patch, grew lumpers. They were what there was to eat. Lumpers for breakfast; lumpers at midday; and if an exhausted Irishman coming home from a long day cutting peat was very lucky, there would still be lumpers left for supper.

Ireland was no stranger to hunger. Every year, in the poorer precincts, the previous season's potato crop would begin running out in July and August, a good month or two before the new autumn crop could be pulled from the ground. The warm months, then, brought with them the familiar routine of the summer hunger. Occasionally more serious crop failures would lead to localized outbreaks of starvation. But as he reached his midteens, Michael would experience an event altogether different, something exceptional even by the standards of Ireland's long history of suffering.

The Irish Potato Famine began in September 1845 in the wake of some notably foggy weather passing over the island. The cause was an unusually virulent blight well suited to take advantage of the damp Irish autumn. The airborne fungus (*Phytopthora infestans*) had been carried to England aboard ships sailing from North America, then blown west across the narrow sea to Ireland. It struck initially on the east coast in the area around Dublin before rapidly spreading inland. Unlike previous potato blights, this one would reach every corner of the country, triggering widespread starvation. Unlike previous hungers, this one would not resolve itself with the next season's harvest. Fully half the total potato crop was lost that first year, and matters only got worse, as three of the next four years saw the blight return. By 1850 more than a million Irish had succumbed to famine and its attendant diseases. A million more had fled the country. A quarter of the nation's eight million people seemed to vanish within the span of five years. (Imagine 80 million Americans disappearing by 2016, and you can begin to appreciate the impact.) It would be more than a century before population levels in Ireland reached prefamine levels once again. Even today, tucked away in remote valleys, you can still see tumbledown stone cottages abandoned as starvation emptied the countryside.

Perversely, the infected lumpers, despite their withered leaves, would have seemed edible when first pulled from the soil. But after a couple of days' storage, fermentation would take hold, reducing the potatoes to a slimy, putrefying, nauseatingly reeking mess unfit even for livestock.

Coincidentally, some 70-odd years later, my father would have his own boyhood experience with the stench of rotting potatoes. One summer, when Dad was eight or nine, Jack Reagan, ever on the lookout for ways to improve his lot, always keen for a sweet deal, purchased a boxcar full of second-grade spuds that he intended to resell at a profit. Of course, someone had to separate the good potatoes from the bad, and that chore fell to my father and his older brother, Moon. For several days, with a hot July sun beating down, the two boys sorted potatoes

— salable ones in that pile, those too far gone in another. Finally, overcome by the sweltering heat and stink of rotting tubers, they put all the remaining potatoes in the same bin and threw them away. In his 1965 autobiography, Dad describes the smell — with unconscious historical resonance — as "worse than that of a decaying corpse." Jack evidently made little profit on his venture.

That sort of boyhood experience, unpleasant as it was at the time, makes for a good story years later. What Michael O'Regan and his family were going through, on the other hand, was the kind of experience people spend their lives trying to forget.

It was during the famine that Michael O'Regan began traveling the few miles to Ballyporeen every day to work in its soap factory. His salary may well have been crucial to keeping his family alive. His daily walks back and forth — like most working people of the time, an Irish laborer thought nothing of a 10-mile round trip — would also have given him a vivid picture of his community's devastation. The horrific tales he brought home to share at the end of a working day may eventually have lost their capacity to shock. As the hunger reached into its second and third years, people avoided driving carts along the lanes at night for fear of rolling over the skeletal remains of neighbors. In a country where wood was scarce, bodies were laid to rest in coffins with trapdoor bottoms, accommodations that could be used multiple times.

These were circumstances that would rouse anyone's urge for self-preservation, even if that meant leaving everything familiar behind and striking out for new territory. Michael O'Regan, staring quite literally into the abyss, faced the biggest decision of his young life. His choice, though he could have no such intuition when he made it, would create ripples extending across distance and time that would change the path of history more than a century later.

CHAPTER TWO
OCEANS OF GRASS

In 1849 Michael's mother, Margaret, died at the age of 48; whether starvation or disease was responsible was not recorded. She may have been buried in the graveyard of the Templetenny Church near her home. Perhaps Michael's wages at the soap factory paid for a small headstone. If so, it has long since sunk into the sod. Within three years her husband, Thomas, followed. Michael had apparently seen enough. Like many Irishmen before him, he decamped to England in search of wages decent enough to allow for savings, with a bit left over, no doubt, to send home. The 1851 British census finds Michael Regan (the O' having dropped off somewhere during the passage from Ireland) living at 24 Benley Street in the Peckham district of South London. A glance at the names of the people sharing the residence paints a telling picture: Brady, Barry, O'Brien, Gorman, Cahill. All but one are Irish, most hailing from Tipperary or neighboring County Cork. Most are in their early to midtwenties. Their professions are decidedly working class: blacksmith, milk carrier, bricklayer, stoker. Michael Regan, living among his 12 housemates, men, women, and children, is still listed as being a soap maker. One can imagine them together, gathered on a front stoop or ambling down to the local pub after a hard day's work, there to pick up news and swap stories of the old country, worrying about loved ones left behind.

London's Great Exhibition in 1851 was the precursor to later world's fairs. Wealthy visitors traveled from around the globe to take in the spectacle at the Crystal Palace, a temporary showcase constructed in Hyde Park. Britain under Queen Victoria had reached the apogee of empire, and this was a way of marking its ascendance. It must have been quite a sight for nineteenth-century eyes: the soaring glass walls rising to a domed arcade; the spring sunshine sparkling on a million panes and slanting downward through steel latticework to frost statuary and living trees with light. On display were all the wonders of the age: William Chamberlin, Jr., demonstrated the world's first automatic vote tabulator; Frederick Bakewell was on hand with what amounted to a crude fax machine; and at least some of the thousands of visitors streaming through the various exhibition halls would have been gratified to discover the world's first pay toilets (a penny a visit). Not all inventions would have a bright future: The Tempest Prognosticator — a barometer employing leeches — never quite caught on.

While England celebrated her vast wealth and globe-straddling empire, London's destitute lived lives of squalid deprivation. Millions now packed themselves into teeming slums, many of them, like Michael Regan, refugees from the potato famine. Within a few years, 20 percent of the city's population would be Irish. The crowded conditions led, predictably enough, to outbreaks of diseases associated with poor sanitation. That drinking water was still being obtained from a Thames River that also served as the city's sewer did not improve the situation. To modern sensibilities, living conditions in mid-nineteenth-century London were appalling. For those who fled famine Ireland, they seemed a step up.

Did they meet on a street corner while taking the air one warm summer night? Or did they catch each other's eye while

mingling in the yeasty air of a neighborhood pub? Perhaps they'd even known each
other back in Tipperary. Across the street
from Michael Regan's Benley Street board-
inghouse, at Number 27, lived Catherine
Mulcahy. The same 1851 census in which
we find Michael identifies Catherine as a
"gardener's laborer." It's possible that she'd
been working with her fellow renters at
Number 27: Bridget Croley, John Ronan,
and his sister Ellen — all from County
Cork — as well as the widow, Mary Magey
from Kildare, are also listed as garden-
ers. Another neighbor, 20-year-old Mary
Bryan of Limerick, is quaintly identified
as a "heather picker." Perhaps one of these
friends had introduced Catherine to the
handsome young soap maker across the
street. Whatever the circumstances of their
acquaintance, by late summer of 1851, Michael Regan and Catherine Mulcahy seem
to have fallen for each other — so much so
that Catherine gave birth to their first son,
Thomas, on May 15 of the following year.
Five and a half months after the happy
event, on All Hallow's Eve 1852, they made
things official, marrying at St. George's
Cathedral in Southwark, London. Whether
the presiding priest was wise to the bride's
maternity is unknown.

What did Catherine, who was six years older than Michael, see in her husband? Did she recognize a drive that would take them beyond their present circumstances? Was there a fondness for liquor that caused concern? And what did he see in her? Someone older and a bit wiser? Did he sense her strength? Catherine would become a bulwark for the Reagan family, outliving Michael by some 16 years, seeing out the century and then some, taking care of her own children and their children until her death.

But that would be years into the future. Now, with the optimism of youth, they made plans. There would be no going back to ravaged Ireland — nothing remained for them there. England, too, offered little but grinding labor and scarce hope of escape from poverty. Their future was in America. The frontier there was steadily pushing west, leaving in its wake land newly opened up to farming — land that could be bought relatively cheaply. Passage across the Atlantic, though, was expensive, so they worked and saved what they could, an effort made no easier by the arrival, in May 1854, of another son, John Michael, and a first daughter, Margaret, in April 1856.

Somehow, they managed to raise their

fares. In November 1857 the ship *Joseph Gilchrist* sailed out of Liverpool Harbor bound for New York. Onboard were 196 souls, among them Michael Regan, his wife, Catherine, and their three children. They landed safely on November 27 at Castle Garden on the southern tip of Manhattan. This was the primary disembarkation point — the Ellis Island of its day — for emigrants from Europe. Having satisfied the doctors at the port that they carried no serious communicable diseases, the Regans found themselves alone in the New World. Slavery sympathizer James Buchanan was America's new president. The Civil War was less than three and a half years away.

There was the little matter of getting from New York to central Illinois. Unlike the many Irish emigrants who would eventually populate the large cities of the eastern seaboard, Michael and his wife envisioned themselves under a wide-open sky. Anyone who has seen Martin Scorsese's *Gangs of New York* will recognize the wisdom of this decision. This was not a period of American history marked by excessive fondness for the Irish, who were widely seen as fit only for the most menial tasks.

Gravediggers, sewer rats: If there was

a nasty job to do, give it to an Irishman. Businesses hung signs by their doors: NO DOGS OR IRISH ALLOWED! On the island of Manhattan, Irish gangs like the Dead Rabbits patrolled emigrant neighborhoods like Hell's Kitchen and warred with nativist thugs. New York in the mid-nineteenth century was hardly the best place to raise a young family. Better to head west to farm country — in Michael's case, Fairhaven Township in Carroll County, Illinois.

They likely traveled by train, a steam locomotive. Charles Dickens, riding the American rails just 15 years earlier, captured the — well, Dickensian — ambience of an early railway journey in *American Notes for General Circulation:*

There is a great deal of jolting, a great deal of noise, a great deal of wall, not much window, a locomotive engine, a shriek, and a bell. The cars are like shabby omnibuses, but larger: holding thirty, forty, fifty people. The seats, instead of stretching from end to end, are placed crosswise. Each seat holds two persons. There is a long row of them on each side of the caravan, a narrow passage up the middle, and a door at both ends. In the centre of the carriage there is usually a stove, fed with charcoal or anthracite coal; which is for the most part red-hot. It is insufferably close; and you see the hot air fluttering between yourself and any other you may happen to look at, like the ghost of smoke.

The children would have drawn pictures on the foggy windows, peered through smudged portholes as wooded hillsides gave way to winter pastures. On to Chicago, the rank ammonia smell of stockyards distinguishing another strange, bustling city they would hasten to leave; then another train steaming them across a rolling prairie where settlements thinned as they traveled due west. Michael and Catherine would have recognized fertile farmland when they saw it, but, unlike the narrower confines of their native Tipperary, the horizon here must have struck them as limitless, the fields, unbounded by centuries of stone walls, impossibly large. To the children, raised in crowded London, the northern Illinois grassland had to be a wonder, a heaving, bounding ocean of earth unimaginable in scope. Too young to understand the enormity of their move, its permanence, the risks involved, did they nevertheless sense their parents' anxiety? Christmas was approaching by the time they reached Fairhaven.

Tracking one's ancestors has become much easier in the past few years. A surging interest in things genealogical has led to a number of Web sites offering access to billions of public records. Seemingly every county and small town in America now has its own history-themed Web site, often featuring cemetery records, among other sources of information. Searches that used to require laborious spelunking into troves of official documents can now be accomplished at home with a few mouse clicks. The deep past comes streaming to life via that most modern of appliances, the computer.

It is, of course, a lot harder to find an ancestor amid this wealth of data if you don't know how they spelled their name — or if they couldn't spell at all. In the 1829 parish registry of Ballyporeen, Thomas, Margaret, and their children are recorded as the "O'Regan" family. Michael, as was often the case for Irish emigrants, dropped the O' when he left Ireland; the 1851 British census and the passenger list from the ship *Joseph Gilchrist* have him as "Regan." The 1860 U.S. Census, however, spells it "Reigan," while also noting that Catherine is illiterate. By 1870, we are entitled to suspect complete inattention on the part of the assistant marshal who appears to have filled out the census form, as the family is now identified as the "Keagans." By 1880, we're somewhat back on track — the name comes out "Ragan" when Michael and Catherine are counted, but, at last, as "Reagan" when referring to their son John, my father's grandfather, who by then was married and living on his own. (From here on, for simplicity's sake, I will use the name Reagan when referring to any family member.)

There is plenty more to be gleaned from census records. In the 1860 count we find that Michael and Catherine have some new arrivals in the house. Their youngest son, William, is just three months old. Michael's older brothers, Nicholas and John, are also present, having followed him over from Ireland. Listed as farm laborers, they appear to be working for their younger brother. Michael's property is valued at $1,120, a sum that compares favorably with the estimates of nearby farms. But his personal estate is only $150, far less than even his poorest neighbor. Michael appears to have sunk all his savings into his land. In the two and a half years since arriving in Fairhaven, he would have needed to build a house and barn, purchase a team of horses, picked up a plow, a harrow, other farming implements, and enough seed to get him started, all the while keeping his family fed.

His strategy seems to have paid off, though, if modestly. By 1870 his holdings are valued at $3,000, and his personal wealth has climbed to $850. Another daughter, Mary, has arrived and reached the age of five. All of his children are attending school. His brothers have by this time struck out on their own. The Civil War has come and gone far to the south and east. Though there were strenuous recruitment efforts among Illinois's young men, there is no evidence that anyone in the Reagan family came anywhere near seeing action or even enlisting. In the meantime, a president hailing from their adopted home state, Abraham Lincoln, has almost single-handedly kept the Union together before being assassinated at Ford's Theater in Washington, D.C. It will be another 110 years before another Illinois native takes up residence in the White House.

By 1880 we see that Michael and Catherine's eldest sons have also left the nest. John had, in 1878, married Jennie Cusick of Dixon, Illinois. The following year, at the age of 25, he is sworn in as an American citizen. He is, at this point, living to the west of his parents' farm in Fulton, Illinois, on the banks of the Mississippi, working in a grain elevator. John and Jennie will eventually have two daughters and two sons, the younger of whom, John Edward ("Jack"), is my grandfather.

It is hard to resist a bit of interpretation when looking at the names of John's children. Irish custom at the time was for first-born sons and daughters to be named after their paternal grandparents. Michael Reagan followed this habit, naming his eldest children Thomas and Margaret. John, however, while naming his older daughter Catherine after his mother, found some reason not to name either of his sons after his father. Was this a case of bad blood between father and son? We will probably never know. John's early death seems to have precluded any such family lore from being passed on.

The decade of the 1880s was not particularly kind to the family. On October 8, 1883, Michael and Catherine's youngest son, William, dies from tuberculosis. The following year, Michael, the patriarch, dies at the age of 55; the cause listed on his death certificate is "congestion of the lungs." On November 19, 1886, his son John's wife, Jennie — my father's grandmother — dies of tuberculosis. John will die of the same disease on January 10, 1889, leaving his four children orphaned. At a Fourth of July picnic that year, his eldest brother, Thomas, drowns. William and Thomas — but apparently not John — are interred with their father in Fulton's Catholic cemetery. My grandfather, Jack, only six at the time, watches as his world falls apart. Michael Reagan's widow, 65-year-old Catherine Reagan, who can neither read nor write, and who has now buried three sons, is left in charge of her two remaining daughters and John's four orphaned children.

On January 25, 1866, in Clyde Township — not more than a couple of miles south of the Reagans' Fairhaven home — another branch of the Reagan family, my father's mother's side, was evolving. A 22-year-old farmer named Thomas Wilson, perhaps even more ambitious than Michael Reagan, married an English emigrant from Surrey, Mary Ann Elsey. On the Illinois prairie of the mid-nineteenth century, marriages rated as news, and this one was taking place on what amounted to neighboring farmland. Word must have reached the Reagan household. If Thomas and Mary threw a celebratory party, the Reagans may even have been guests.

Thomas was a lifelong resident of Clyde, his father, John Wilson of Paisley, Scotland, having moved there in 1839, just as the remaining Native Americans were being driven west across the Mississippi River. One of his brothers is said to have starved while on a mining expedition to Colorado's Pikes Peak; another allegedly survived by eating the flesh of a dead companion. A photograph taken at a somewhat later age shows Thomas as a well-dressed, dark-haired man with a flamboyant mustache and goatee into which a bit of salt has crept to join the pepper. He radiates an air of confidence, having by that time become a very successful farmer. He has also taken to spending extended periods of time away from home. His wife, Mary, in a contemporaneous photo, strikes the viewer as a woman accustomed to heartache. Clad in black, sad-eyed, her mouth a tense line, she seems the very image of a good-hearted, God-fearing pioneer woman destined to be disappointed by her man.

Whatever demons may have troubled Thomas, the unmistakable impression is that something went very wrong in the Wilson marriage. In a picture taken in 1898, Mary, clad in black, sits surrounded by her seven children. Toothless and wizened, she is all of 55 years old. By 1900, even though Thomas won't be dead for another nine years, Mary is calling herself a widow. Being separated from each other for all that time must have taken its toll. The couple is even buried in separate cemeteries — Mary in the town of Fulton, where she rests next to a daughter, Jennie, who died of a cerebral hemorrhage; Thomas, so the story goes, buried by a son next to his parents in a tiny plot near his farm in Clyde.

Traveling back to Illinois in order to see firsthand the places connected to my father and his family, I decide to make a foray into the country farmed by Thomas Wilson and, just a few miles north, Michael Reagan. I want to get some feel for the land, but, more specifically, I want to locate the grave of my grandmother Nelle's father, the man who seems to have abandoned his wife and family.

Most people, even many of those who have investigated my father's past, characterize the north-central Illinois prairie as flat, confusing its topography, perhaps, with that of other areas of the Midwest. While there are level stretches — around Tampico, for instance — much of the landscape is less a chessboard than a series of gently rolling mounds, most plowed, some left topped by copses of trees. Over and around these I drive, following the generally gridlike pattern of roads, some paved, some dirt. According to a record of my family published by dentist and amateur genealogist Curt Gronner, Thomas Wilson is buried in the "North Clyde Cemetery." A similar clue, arriving serendipitously from a third cousin I'd never met, indicates Thomas's youngest son, Alexander, interred his father "privately." I've managed to spot what looks to be a likely plot in the area using Google Earth, and I head in what I hope is the right direction. It turns out to be someone's backyard. By sheer luck, though, I stumble across some headstones a quarter mile or so farther on. Leaving my rental car parked in the grass by the side of the road, and with a growing sense of anticipation, I walk up a gentle slope and begin scanning the markers. No Thomas.

I return to the car, feeling a bit deflated, for more driving around. For the fourth time I wave to the same farmer on his tractor as I pass by. I try the local Methodist Church — Thomas was a Scots Protestant — but no one is around. Finally, abandoning my male aversion to asking for directions, I pull into a farmhouse near the original cemetery. An aging cattle-dog shifts himself from his station at a side door and comes growling my way. As I attempt rapprochement with the security force, a voice calls, "Can I help you?" The farmer in residence is standing on his front porch. Once I've explained myself, he directs me to a plot not far up the road — I must have just missed it on my first, second, and third passes. Sure enough, inscribed on a modest yet not insubstantial marker are the names of Thomas's parents, John and Jane. Thomas's name, however, appears nowhere. A later Web search indicates he is, indeed, buried there, but apparently none of his family thought enough of him to pitch in for a headstone, or even for an inscription on the existing monument.

However strained the marriage between Thomas and Mary became, however seldom Thomas was around, he evidently visited often enough over the years to sire seven children, the youngest of whom was Nelle Clyde Wilson, my father's mother.

Given that their farms were within walking — or at least easy riding — distance, it seems quite plausible that the Reagan and Wilson families were at least acquainted, perhaps for decades. They may have looked on with sympathy or dismay as each family endured its share of tribulations. In any case, they seem to have moved along parallel paths.

With Thomas having taken himself out of

the picture, Mary Wilson moved with her children to Fulton, where Catherine Reagan had also moved with her brood one year after the death of her husband, Michael. Catherine's daughters, Margaret and Mary, opened a millinery shop on Fourth Street, the town's main thoroughfare. Mary, the younger by eight years, would wed first and have two children before being widowed. In 1894, Margaret married Orson G. Baldwin, a dry goods merchant, and moved to Bennett, Iowa, taking her nephew, Jack, with them. They soon moved back to Fulton, though, to help care for Catherine, who was becoming increasingly infirm. Baldwin set up a dry goods store there as well and continued to employ Jack, whose formal education had ended at the elementary level, as a clerk. Though it's uncertain, he might even have hired Thomas and Mary Wilson's auburn-haired daughter, Nelle, too, when brisk business warranted. It would not be until 1904, though, that the orphaned Jack Reagan would ask Nelle for her hand in marriage — two young people from fractured homes hoping to find security and solace in each other.

Together, they would struggle and prosper modestly, battle and reconcile, pick up stakes often, and, along the way, produce two sons, the younger of whom would become, first, a radio sportscaster, then a moderately famous Hollywood actor, and finally, the forty-fourth president of the United States.

CHAPTER THREE
THE STORY BEGINS

He arrived noisily, feet first and flushed an alarming shade of blue. At 4:16 A.M. on February 6, 1911, after 24 grueling hours of labor, Nelle Wilson Reagan gave birth to her second child in the small second-floor apartment above a bakery in Tampico, Illinois, that she shared with her husband, Jack, and their two-year-old firstborn, Moon (his nickname taken from a cartoon character of the day, "Moon Mullins"). The cries of the newly arrived 10-pound boy filled the tiny bedroom, its west-facing windows overlooking Main Street still blank with winter darkness. Carrying out into the predawn silence, the sound might have awakened a few neighbors, who felt relief at hearing such a healthy yowl emerge from the Reagan home. Presumably they waited until sunup to inquire after the health of the mother. Only the day before, Tampico had been buried in such a heavy snow that train service had been

72

suspended till the tracks could be cleared. Fortunately, Nelle's doctor, who lived just a few blocks down the street, was not averse to kicking his way through a few drifts on behalf of a patient in need. Mindful of the strain imposed by labor on her small body, he would advise Nelle to have no more children.

Jack, who later admitted being rendered bloodless by the ordeal, looked gratefully at his squalling new son and asked, "For such a little bit of a fat Dutchman, he makes a hell of a lot of noise, doesn't he?" Exhausted, auburn hair matted with sweat, Nelle offered a more decisive appraisal: "He's perfectly wonderful." Then she pronounced his name: "Ronald Wilson Reagan." It had almost been "Donald," after a great grandfather in her father's Wilson line, but one of Nelle's sisters had beat her to it. So Ronald Reagan it was — a name that has now joined a select pantheon blessed or cursed with instant recognition and powerful associations. But for the first quarter century or so of my father's long, eventful life, it was Jack's handle that stuck. Until he moved to California and a career on the silver screen, everyone but his mother would call him "Dutch."

The town's newspaper, the *Tampico Tornado,* while noncommittal on the issue of his name, duly registered the birth of the town's newest citizen and the joyful relief of his father: "John Reagan has been calling thirty-seven inches a yard and giving seventeen ounces for a pound this week at Pitney's store he has been feeling so jubilant over the arrival of a ten pound boy Monday."

In the East Room of the Washington, D.C. residence in which little Dutch would eventually spend eight years hangs a portrait of George Washington by Gilbert Stuart. In 1814, as British troops moved to sack the capital, First Lady Dolley Madison, having been urged by her husband to evacuate, famously spirited the painting to safety. The work's intrinsic value as portraiture never interested Dad nearly as much as the cinematic derring-do of its narrow escape. "Picture her here all alone in the house with the British coming down the road," he would muse, head cocked left, his voice growing ever so slightly husky, the twinkle in his eyes acquiring just a hint of mist, as they did whenever he recounted tales of personal courage.

As she prepared to abandon the White House — but not George — to the invaders, Dolley penned a description of events to her sister, Anna:

Our kind friend, Mr. Carroll, has come to hasten my departure, and in a very bad humor with me, because I insist on waiting until the large picture of General Washington is secured, and it requires to be unscrewed from the wall. This process was found to be too tedious for these perilous moments; I have ordered the frame to be broken, and the canvas taken out. It is done! [A]nd the precious portrait placed in the hands of two gentlemen from New York, for safe keeping. And now, dear sister, I must leave this house, or the retreating army will make me a prisoner in it by filling up the road I am directed to take. When I shall again write to you, or where I shall be to-morrow, I cannot tell!

"Imagine that!" I can still see Dad's face, filled with wonder at such selfless courage.

It startles me to realize that my father's entrance into the world was closer in time to Dolley Madison's hurriedly penned note than to my typing these words on a computer — a device as unimaginable to a juvenile Dutch as it would have been to James Madison's stalwart wife. The shootout at the O.K. Corral was barely as distant from the scene in that narrow Tampico bedroom as Ronald Reagan's first inaugural is from us today. George Armstrong Custer's demise at the Little Bighorn was only six years further in the past than Dad's portrayal of a young Custer in *Santa Fe Trail* was in the future.

Dutch, of course, could have no firsthand knowledge of the wild West, Indian Wars, or prairie hardship, no personal sense of a limitless frontier opening toward the sunset, let alone any appreciation for the horrors of the Irish famine. But all that and more was within his family's living memory. His great-grandmother, Catherine Reagan of Tipperary, resided until 1905 in the river town of Fulton, only 25 miles to the northwest. Illiterate though she was, there was nothing to keep her from sharing stories of her early life with her grandson Jack, whom she raised for a time after his father died. It seems impossible that at least some of these tales of hunger, a ship's passage to a new world, and life on the Illinois grasslands a half century before wouldn't have circulated through the Reagan household as my father grew up. If so, he declined, for unknown reasons, to share them with his own family.

My father arrived, if you will, between acts. By the calendar, the nineteenth century may have ended a decade earlier; culturally speaking, it had not quite drawn to a close. The twentieth century was visible in the promise of myriad new technologies, but for ordinary Americans it still shimmered just beyond reach. Had you been able to cross America in a high-flying jet back in 1911, you would have peered down at a distinctly unfamiliar country. At just over 90 million citizens, the nation's population was less than a third that of today. People were spread more evenly across the landscape; most still lived on farms or in small rural towns not unlike Tampico. Though railroads had long since connected the coasts, the absence of interstate highways, with their looping cloverleafs and rivers of traffic, would be striking. The automotive age had only just gotten rolling. Buggy whips were giving way to ignition cranks, but the unpaved streets of country towns were still plied by horse-drawn carts. No one needed a driver's license. Most people's only experience of air travel would have been barnstormers in biplanes. The breeze hadn't yet acquired the reek of petrochemicals we take for granted; it carried instead the grassy smell of horse droppings and, particularly in winter, the distinctive tang of coal smoke billowing up chimneys from the fires used to heat most homes.

Modern refrigeration did not yet exist; iceboxes were supplied by horse-drawn wagons loaded with frozen blocks cut from nearby rivers. Clothes were washed by hand and hung outside to dry. Milk cost $0.32 a gallon. The average salary was $750 a year. (If you were a Ziegfeld girl, however, you could pull in $75 per week.)

In 1911, disk phonographs were only just replacing wax cylinders as the new Victrolas became popular. There were still no regular radio broadcasts. Not until the 1920s would my father and a few boyhood friends listen, transfixed, as a voice seemed to materialize from the air: "This is KDKA Pittsburgh . . . This is KDKA Pittsburgh . . ." While kinetoscopes provided novelty entertainment with their jerky, stuttering images, "talking pictures" would wait another 15 years for the premiere of the Warner Bros. production *Don Juan*.

Men wore starched collars, straw boaters, and derbies; fashionable women promenaded beneath the sweeping confections of Gainsborough hats. The U.S. president at the time, William Howard Taft, sported a walrus mustache. (He would be the last president to display any facial hair.)

Should you take your time-traveling overflight at night, you would also be impressed by the darkness. Thomas Edison had invented his electric lightbulb 32 years before, and many already brightened the main streets of large cities, but the agrarian countryside was still lit mostly by fire. There was no continentwide electrical grid. Tampico, as it happened, was among the first of Illinois's rural towns to generate its own electrical power. The Reagans would have lived under the stark glare of the early incandescent bulbs, with oil lamps used for backup. Indoor plumbing was another matter. Down a steep flight of wooden stairs descending from a screened sleeping porch at the rear of the Reagan apartment was a pump that supplied water necessary for drinking, cooking, and bathing. An outhouse, frigid in winter, ripe in summer, was also located there.

The year of my father's birth, Roald Amundsen became the first person to reach the South Pole, while his chief competitor, Robert Falcon Scott, entered the annals of tragedy. Jack Johnson, to the outrage of many white boxing fans of the day, remained the world's heavyweight champion, having defeated Great White Hope Jim Jeffries the year before. Babe Ruth was still a schoolboy athlete, belting home runs at St. Mary's Industrial School for Boys.

The HMS *Titanic* rested in dry dock, still imagined to be unsinkable.

The world was a quieter place, the daily

round for most folks less hectic. It is tempting to consider America in the years surrounding the turn of the century as representative of a vanished Golden Age. But life then could also be hard and pitiless. Those nostalgic for the charms of this bygone era might want to consider the realities of sickness and death. As a male, Dutch Reagan had a life expectancy at birth, according to actuarial statistics, of less than 50 years; women fared little better. Smallpox, tuberculosis, diphtheria, and polio had yet to be eradicated. There were no antibiotics. Surgery was crude, dentistry a form of sanctioned torture. People commonly perished due to diseases that today could be easily treated or cured. As a young boy, my father looked on helplessly as his mother nearly died of the flu.

Yet people could feel a transformation coming. The steady accretion of technological advances over the previous decades foretold comforts and advantages that would usher in new ways of living, even if it would take a few more years for them to reach small-town America. Like many women of her generation, Nelle Reagan would have looked forward to a life of far less exhausting drudgery than her mother had endured.

Social relationships were changing as well.

The populism of the late nineteenth century was morphing into a new progressivism. The decade following my father's birth would mark the apogee of the women's suffrage movement, culminating with passage of the Nineteenth Amendment in 1920. The year he was born, the Supreme Court would find the Standard Oil Company in violation of the Sherman Antitrust Act. This year, 1911, was also the one in which 146 people, most of them young women, locked in an upper-story sweatshop at the Triangle Shirtwaist Company in New York, would perish in a blaze, a preventable tragedy that further galvanized the labor movement. Race relations, too, were a foremost topic of discussion. Booker T. Washington had published *Up from Slavery* 10 years earlier. The NAACP had been formed in 1909. Meanwhile, in Okemah, Oklahoma, a black woman alleged to have shot a sheriff was seized by vigilantes, gang-raped, and lynched, one of 60 known black American lynching victims that year. In the early years of the twentieth century, old savageries mingled jarringly with modernizing impulses.

Progressive currents did not bypass the Reagan household. Jack may have valued hard work and self-reliance, but he was also aware of darker forces in the world willing to

81

enforce social hierarchies based on race and class as a means of maintaining power. Jack was an enthusiastic member of the Democratic Party and had a particular disdain for bigotry of any flavor. When D. W. Griffith's *Birth of a Nation* opened in 1915, Jack refused to take his wife and children. "It deals with the Ku Klux Klan against the colored folks, and I'm damned if anyone in this family will go see it," my father recalls him saying. Though Jack was in many ways Nelle's polar opposite, his abhorrence of injustice would have resonated harmoniously with his wife's burgeoning Christian sensibilities. She had been baptized as a member of the Disciples of Christ Church the year before my father was born, one more step in a personal progression of piety. Following the teachings of her church, she, too, rejected distinctions based on race or creed — her husband's nominal Catholicism clearly proving no impediment to their marriage, even though her denomination was well-known for its hostility to the papacy. She was convinced, so my father later put it, that "everyone loved her just because she loved them."

Leaving Fulton, Illinois, where Jack and Nelle met and married, crossing the Rock River from Sterling into Rock Falls, I follow a narrow ribbon of asphalt south toward Tampico. The landscape, varied and rolling north of the river, flattens out here. (In the late 1850s, when Tampico was founded, the terrain was boggy and rather inhospitable to farming.) Trees flanking the Hennepin Canal, which, since the early years of the twentieth century has drawn water from the Rock to irrigate farms in the area, are visible to the east, running parallel to the highway. This early in May the surrounding fields are a mix of freshly turned earth, new crops sprouting, and the stubble of last season's cornstalks. The air is loud with the hum of insects. Red-winged blackbirds busy themselves along the roadsides. The typical rural carnage is on display: Raccoons and opossums, struck by cars, are left bloating at the margins of the pavement.

Though the afternoon is settling toward evening by the time I reach Tampico, the spring sun is still well above the horizon. Its rays warm the two-story red-brick facades of the storefronts along the east side of Main Street, so familiar to me after hours spent examining old photos of their earlier incarnations. Feeling a bit conspicuous — I seem to be the only one out and about — I pull up to the building that formerly housed the H. C. Pitney store and park the car. I find the front door locked; the building is apparently no longer in use. The windows, which once enticed farmers and their wives with displays of the latest shoes, hats, and suits, are boarded over with only small rectangular peepholes allowing a view into their present jumbled interiors. The striped pole, which used to occupy a prominent place on the sidewalk out front, has long since disappeared. Standing in the spot where my grandfather Jack appears in the photo I'd first seen at the Reagan Library, I gaze out across the street as he once did. In my mind's eye, images of Tampico today mingle interchangeably with the Tampico of a century past.

John Backlund's sign, with its cartoon cannon blasting high prices, has vanished along with the building from which it hung. Likewise the hardware store and tailor shop, with its lunchroom. Main Street, these days properly (if not recently) paved, is no longer a muddy morass. But it is hard to escape the impression of decline. Gone are the ranks of carriages and wagons busily ferrying farmers and their families to market day. Mine is one of only three cars parked in the town's center. The population, over 1,200 at the time of my father's birth, has dwindled to fewer than 800. How long has it been since Main Street's sidewalks were noisy with bustling crowds of shoppers? Tampico, like so many small farm towns, has clearly seen more prosperous days. In fact, the village was arguably approaching its zenith just about the time the Reagan family arrived.

It may be hard to imagine now why a dynamic, driven young man like Jack Reagan would, in March of 1906, decamp with his young wife from his larger hometown of Fulton, trading a bustling port on the Mississippi River for the relatively bucolic environs of Tampico. But Tampico in those days was something more than a backwater. It boasted a train line, courtesy of the Chicago, Burlington and Quincy Railroad. The nearby Hennepin Canal was nearing completion, a boon for local farmers, and what was good for the farmers was good for the merchants who supplied their needs. A succession of fires and tornadoes over the previous decades had repeatedly assaulted the town's main thoroughfare, reducing its clapboard structures to kindling and ashes, but new brick buildings had gone up in their places, including the one H. C. Pitney would buy for his dry goods emporium. Tampico, in those years, was a place where eager, energetic young people like Jack and Nelle could make their mark.

Though only 23 years old, Jack already

had years of experience in retail sales, having worked since his teenage years for his aunt Margaret and her husband in their dry goods stores in Bennett, Iowa, and later in Fulton. When H. C. Pitney offered him a position as senior salesman in the clothing and shoe department of his new business — the largest such store in the area — Jack was keen for the opportunity. Possessed of what his younger son would later refer to as "burning ambition," Jack would have cut a striking figure among the bib-overalled rustics of Tampico. Somehow this orphaned progeny of rough-hewn Irish immigrants had acquired in his brief life a cosmopolitan sheen. Smartly dressed, well groomed, and always ready with an endless repertoire of jokes and stories — some of them bawdy, as the occasion warranted — he made a positive impression as a young man with prospects. He took the shoe business seriously, studying diligently to become a "licensed practipedist," developing expertise in the new technique of using X-ray machines to fit his wares to customers' feet. He may have had second thoughts about his move when Tampico outlawed liquor the year after his arrival, but once he convinced his new boss to purchase a Model T for buying trips, Chicago — and its drinking establishments — came well within range.

Nelle, too, left an indelible impression on her adopted community. Far from being overshadowed by her husband's blarney-spouting effervescence, if anything she seemed to thrive on the competition. Demure in appearance, she was by nature a dynamo. The Reagan family may have had two generals, but Nelle was the one wearing five stars.

Jack and Nelle had been wed in the rectory of Fulton's Immaculate Conception Church, as church rules prohibited Jack from marrying a non-Catholic at the altar. After the birth of her first son, Moon, in Tampico, she was visited by the local priest, who sternly reminded her that, as a condition of her marriage, she had agreed to raise her children as Catholics, meaning Moon must be baptized as such forthwith. Nelle, the daughter of a Methodist, protested that she had agreed to no such thing. The priest glowered, but Jack, a more devoted husband than churchgoer, came to her rescue. It had been his responsibility to secure this agreement with his bride-to-be and, knowing her temperament as he did, he had conveniently "forgotten." In the end Nelle relented and allowed the Catholic baptism to be performed. By the time of Ronald's birth, however, she had stiffened her religious spine.

There would be no further compromise with the Catholic Church. Her second son would be brought up to make his own decisions regarding religion, period.

Nelle's faith seems to have undergone a florescence sometime between the births of her two sons. Though her name's first appearance on the membership rolls of Tampico's Christian Church, a branch of the Disciples of Christ, is undated, it appears she was baptized into the denomination in 1910. Nelle would have professed her devotion to Jesus Christ as her personal savior, as is the case in most Protestant sects, but her new religious community was more interested in deeds than words. The Disciples were a liberal church. This was activist (you might even say socialist) Christianity; adherents were expected to express their faith through good works in the wider world. This suited my energetic grandmother to a T.

At the Reagan Library I came across a poem written by Nelle. (She was still spelling her name Nellie at the time, but later dropped the I, feeling that the new spelling was more dignified; I have used that version of her name throughout to avoid confusion.) Entitled "A Sonnet," it offers a clear idea of her religious sensibilities:

When I consider how my life is spent
The most that I can do will be to prove
'Tis by his side, each day, I seek to move.
To higher, nobler things my mind is bent
Thus giving of my strength, which God has
  lent,
I strive some needy souls unrest, to soothe
Lest they the paths of righteousness shall
  lose
Through fault of mine, my Maker to present.
If I should fail to show them of this need
How could I hope to meet him face to face,
Or give a just account of all my ways
In thought of mind, in word, and in each
  deed
My life must prove the power of His grace
By every action through my living days.

Nelle would strive to soothe the unrest of needy souls throughout her life. During her younger and middle-aged years, she regularly visited local jails to read to prisoners, sometimes persuading the sheriff to allow them a visit to her home, where she would serve them a meal before sending them off with an admonition to "do good." In later years, after she had moved to Los Angeles to be near her sons, she shifted her attention to patients at a hospital for sufferers of tuberculosis and, in a pinch, any down and out homeless people she happened across. My parents would occasionally drop by her small home to find a complete stranger — some unfortunate she had encountered on her rounds — enjoying a bite of lunch. She was the sort of generous spirit whom traveling hobos in years past would favor with an appreciative inscription on the gatepost: A GOOD WOMAN LIVES HERE.

I step down from the threshold of the old Pitney Store and begin angling across the street toward the apartment at 111 South Main Street, now marked by a plaque identifying it as my father's birthplace. Out of habit, I look both ways. No need; traffic is nonexistent. Next door to the birthplace is a related museum. Inside, two older men are seated at a small table. "Are you guys in charge here?" I ask, not bothering to introduce myself. For most of my life — certainly since realizing that my name alone could produce a great deal of curiosity and consternation — I've been cautious about throwing "Reagan" around when meeting strangers for fear of conveying any impression of grandiosity or entitlement, and because of a general disinclination to cause a fuss. It's silly but reflexive, and occasionally leads to awkward moments.

"My wife really runs the place," says the gentleman nearest to me. "You want to take the tour?"

"Sure do."

"Well, before we go upstairs to the birthplace," he says, rising from his chair, "let me bring you over to the window and point out a few things." I dutifully follow him to the front of the room facing the street. "See that building across the way with the red brick?" he asks. "Now that . . . ," he pauses to signal the impending arrival of significant information," . . . was the H. C. Pitney Store."

At this point I realize the jig is up; in order to spare both of us senseless embarrassment, my little charade of anonymity must cease. "My grandfather used to work in that store," I tell him.

He regards me with something not unlike suspicion. "Your granddad was . . . H. C. Pitney?"

"No, my grandfather was Jack Reagan." The poor fellow's eyes begin to widen, and I plunge ahead. "My father was born in that apartment upstairs. My name is Ron Reagan."

"Oh, my goodness," he says, slowly shaking his head. "Oh, my goodness. Here I am telling you these things, and you ought to be telling me!"

In short order his wife is summoned, along with Joan Johnson, who coordinates tours. We peruse some of the photos and other artifacts on display. I pull out my laptop and insert a CD to show them the old photograph of Jack standing in the doorway of the Pitney store. Joan reminds me that I've actually been to Tampico before, as a teenager working on my father's 1976 presidential campaign. Due to swing through the area by bus, Dad had expressed interest in seeing his birthplace. At the time the apartment had yet to be reincarnated as a historical landmark. The couple in residence, who were out of town when my father visited, had kindly agreed to have someone let him in for a look around. With mounting anticipation he arrived at the door, only to find that they had forgotten to leave a key under the mat. It would be 15 years before he would return, no longer an aspirant to the nation's highest office but a former president embarking on the final chapter of his life.

At last Joan asks if I am ready to see the apartment.

Up a narrow flight of stairs is a single door. It opens onto what is described as the "formal dining area." This seems a rather grand way to describe what, at first glance, appears to be little more than an overly large entrance hall. But maybe Jack and Nelle did use the room to feed and entertain friends. Circling the heavy dining table (the furniture is of the correct period but not actual Reagan property), my attention fixes instead on one of the photo blow-ups hanging on the wall. Edmund Morris memorably described the picture in *Dutch,* but I'd never before laid eyes on it.

Jack, Nelle, and a few friends have taken the kids to a nearby swimming hole. Nelle, sitting on some sort of small dock, her legs dangling, leans toward a friend with whom she's enjoying an animated conversation. Lower in the frame, half immersed in the water, Jack trains his impish grin on the camera from between her legs. Moon and Dutch stand in the background, looking as if they've just clambered out after a swim. Their bathing suits are plastered to their skinny frames; my father in particular, with his striped shorts and knobby knees, looks in need of a brisk toweling off.

Dad may appear in more photographs than anyone since the medium was invented The movie business contributed reams of publicity stills. Then, for eight years, he was tailed on a daily basis by at least one official White House photographer, who could be counted on to chronicle everything from summit meetings to a lunchtime bowl of soup. Few of these images pique my interest. Early pictures, though, especially casual snapshots like this one from his childhood, exert a profound fascination — like a portal allowing time travel.

None of the people captured in this photo is still alive; their world, that moment, even the memory of it, have vanished with them. Yet here they are: Dad in his sopping shirt; his still young parents and brother; their anonymous friends — frozen in time. The particulars of that day — the sunshine cascading down, the rustling of leaves and trilling of birds in the trees above, the water eddying beneath their feet as they rest on the rough boards of the dock — once all made up the present moment, as real and immediate as my fingers now touching this keyboard. Air wafting the scent of earth and grass; light splashing across pale shoulders, just so. That little boy fumbling with the buttons of his shirtfront will one day become my father — and ultimately an iconic figure to millions — but in this instant, through this magic window to the past, he is once more little Dutch, shivering and goosefleshed in a summer breeze.

We finish the tour: the tiny, light-filled

front room where Dad's birth took place — a bed and night table on which a lamp sits the only furniture — Jack and Nelle's bedroom in the apartment's interior, windowless but for a skylight that Nelle disliked, Joan tells me, because it let in flashes of lightning during thunderstorms; the kitchen, with its woodstove and icebox; a window off the sleeping porch that opens into the apartment next door, and through which Nelle and her neighbor would pass their infants back and forth as they swapped babysitting duties. I inhale the old-house smell and peer out a front window — as Nelle would have — in the direction of the Pitney store. The apartment has been conscientiously restored despite a shoestring budget — I feel a twinge of guilt for not bringing a checkbook. Yet while I'm grateful for the opportunity to spend a few moments here, to finally see the spot where my father came into the world, my mind keeps returning to that image hanging in the front room: the Reagan family at play on that distant summer day.

Apart from the photo at the swimming hole, only a handful of snapshots and a few studio portraits provide a visual record of the family's early years. In one of the earliest, my father is an infant, dressed in white, chortling and reaching a chubby right hand toward the camera as if in eager anticipation of their long and fruitful relationship to come. All his physical trademarks are present in nascent form: Nelle's straight brow line; Jack's thick head of hair; his own crooked grin. Brother Moon hovers behind him, a quizzical look on his face, as if already perplexed to find himself dwelling in the shadows cast by this new arrival's glow.

How odd it is to look at such a picture — my father so alien in his infancy, yet, at the same time, so recognizable. Accustomed to seeing Dad in his mature role of patriarch and protector, I find it slightly unnerving to confront evidence of his vulnerable fragility. From my vantage point a century on, I have seen his beginning, middle, and end. Cooing, cornstarched, exuding baby musk in some long-vanished photographer's studio, he sees in the world nothing but a reflection of his own innocence. In a rush of tenderness I want to catch him up in my arms and place him somewhere safe, beyond anger and disappointment. Can't we banish everything but kindness and grace from this child's life? It is a feeling I recognize from his last years, watching him as he spiraled toward a state not unlike infancy.

In a photograph from a year or so later we find the family together in their Sunday best. An unknown portraitist has dragged what may be an ottoman across scuffed wooden floorboards and draped it with a tasseled throw. On it the two youngsters perch. Moon is wearing what looks like a new suit — short pants still, but over them a tweed jacket the hem of which he clutches with sartorial satisfaction. That pride in appearance he may already have picked up from his father. Jack stands over his shoulder, too handsome by half for a life in the boondocks. Splendid in a dark three-piece suit — jacket buttoned, vest barely visible beneath; uncuffed trousers breaking just so over brightly polished shoes — he looks confident and relaxed. Broad shoulders squared, chest flat and wide, he holds his arms relaxed at his sides. His right hand curls into a loose fist with thick veins prominent behind the knuckles — a minor physical trait that will be passed on through two more generations. A starched white collar and white necktie set off a complexion his younger son will later describe as "swarthy." Parted down the middle, his hair executes a flamboyant swoop above his left brow. On the other side of the ottoman stands Nelle. Her dense hair is swept back. She is dressed in light-colored, floor-length crepe, the toes of her shoes peek out from beneath the hem of her dress. Her face wears its usual expression: a mixture of kindness and vague concern. She is by no means unattractive, but with her sharp chin and earnest demeanor, it is unlikely anyone ever called her beautiful behind her back. Pressed to her right hip, grinning in a white smock and dimpling cherubically, is my toddling father. His hair is cut in a Dutch-boy bob. His little black shoes have yet to see enough use to become scuffed. In a few years he will acquire a more somber demeanor. But at this early juncture, he seems lit from within.

Among their fellow residents, the Reagans of Tampico would have qualified as bohemians of a sort (not to mention progressives, freethinkers, and Democrats in a countryside stocked with conservative Republicans). Nelle, for one, couldn't have delighted in churchgoing any more than she loved performing in local theatrical productions at Burden's Opera House, across the street from their original apartment. Jack, a ham more in the raconteur mode, supported his wife's acting, treading the boards alongside her with gusto often enough that they became the Lunt and Fontanne of the northern Illinois farm set.

When babysitters were unavailable on rehearsal days, Nelle would, so the story goes, bring baby Dutch to the theater with her, setting him down near the footlights where she could keep an eye on him. It's tempting to imagine that he absorbed during these interludes his love of acting, but he retained no such infant memories. Not until the family returned to Tampico some years later would Nelle press him into theatrical service. But by then, the setting would be her church and the scripts of a decidedly more devotional nature.

In Tampico's birthplace museum, I pick up a playbill from one of Jack and Nelle's theatrical adventures circa 1913, *A Woman's Honor.* The fact that people from outlying towns apparently thought it worth their while to hop aboard trains and travel to Tampico just for the pleasure of such a performance at least must count as testament to the Reagans' enthusiasm for the stage, if not for their actual acting talent. On Thanksgiving that same year, Nelle would rise to what may have been her greatest theatrical triumph: a triple role — nun, matron, and cotton picker — in *Millie the Quadroon; or, Out of Bondage,* billed as a play of "antebellum trueness." With Jack costarring in blackface, she packed the house and drew rave reviews.

It was in the summer of that heady year that Jack finally convinced H. C. Pitney to spot him the cash for the Model T. Jack had, by that time, established himself in the community. Within three months of my father's birth, the family had moved into a house on Glassburn Street, south of the railroad tracks. It would be the largest home in which they would ever live. Jack was serving as treasurer of the local Catholic Church (probably in lieu of regularly attending mass), volunteering with the fire department, and managing the Pitney store whenever the boss left town. Nelle, too, was active in town, especially with her own church. But Jack was restless. More and more people were getting around in cars. It wouldn't do for Pitney's leading sales representative to be seen thumbing a ride or hanging onto the back of a hay wagon. As the August 21, 1913, issue of the *Tampico Tornado* put it:

A prominent Fairfield township farmer commenting on the fact that the assessor's books show more money invested [in] autos than was on deposit in banks remarks that if he remembered correctly,

Tampico township has $19,460 tied up in autos and only $16,020 in the mortgage lifting hogs, and $19,026 in household furniture showing that Tampico too is getting more money in the buzz wagons than in hogs and household furniture.

Times were indeed changing.

The new Model T plays a starring role in one of my father's earliest memories: Jack is driving the family home from somewhere when he runs the car into a ditch, flipping it upside down and crushing its roof. Dad had a vague but disturbing recollection of being trapped inside and hearing his mother's frantic voice calling his name as she and Jack struggled to free him.

This memory, along with a couple of others from early childhood — Jack coming home from work and nuzzling him with alarmingly bristly chin whiskers; slipping from the seat of a swing and suffering rope burns on his hands — I had never heard while growing up. They were shared, much later, with Edmund Morris, his authorized biographer. Reflecting on that, I try not to feel like a kid who hasn't been invited to the birthday party. After all, I never asked Dad to dredge up his primal recollections. The earliest memories actually volunteered

101

by my father derive from the family's brief sojourn to Chicago, a move that would kick off a six-year-long period of rootless migration.

CHAPTER FOUR
THE TRAVELING REAGANS

"Jack didn't drink when times were tough; he would go on a bender to celebrate when things were going his way." Dad recited this characterization to me countless times during the years I was growing up. His point seemed to be that his father was not flagrantly irresponsible but weak — an Irishman expressing jubilation in a stereotypically Irish way: by disappearing for a few days into a boozy round of tavern hopping before stumbling home to sleep off his hangover. Hard on the heels of this account would come the reminder of Nelle's admonition to her boys about Jack's occasional drunken absences: It was not his fault; he had what amounted to a sickness that he couldn't control; Jack's children should not harbor anger toward their father but remember instead his abundant good qualities.

A generous sentiment, but I suspect Nelle was less forgiving in practice. Many decades later my father would recall hearing "a lot of cursing from my parents' bedroom when my mother went after [Jack] for his drinking." Let me translate that into a more realistic account: Jack and Nelle were having knockdown, drag-out shouting matches that probably woke the neighbors. In any case, as the year 1915 arrived, Jack must have felt things were going very much his way, with all the risk that entailed. He had landed a retail job with a large chain, the Fair Department Store. The family was moving to Chicago, the City of Broad Shoulders — many of which could be found jostling their way toward the bar in any one of the city's thousands of taverns. Windy City citizens of the day were prominent among America's leading consumers of alcohol.

Jack must have felt he had finally broken free of the sticks. Here was a place where he could rise to his natural level, where he would be among people of sophistication. Here, in this crowded, bustling metropolis — the very city his grandparents had likely passed through on their way to a new life on the Illinois prairie nearly 60 years before — he and his family would flourish, reaping the benefits of the onrushing twentieth century.

The magnitude of change swirling around the Reagan family, as all families at that time, must have been astonishing. Serbian nationalist Gavrilo Princip had assassinated Archduke Franz Ferdinand the previous June, setting off World War I; America would ultimately join the fight in 1917, in the process boosting an industrialization that would shortly propel the nation to an unaccustomed status as a global power. Meanwhile, on the home front, the automobile was completing its conquest of the nation's roads, fundamentally altering the average American's sense of time, distance, and travel. Social mores were relaxing, too, especially for women. Everywhere the world seemed in a process of transformation. The very complexion of America was changing as new shiploads of immigrants arrived daily. As during the sixties and again today, the demise of old orders, the overturning of what had seemed to be settled patterns of life, produced anxiety as well as excitement. In timeless and predictable fashion, nativists and social conservatives began reaching for their pitchforks. By the time the Reagans made their move to Chicago, rumblings about Prohibition had begun in earnest, though in 1915, five years before the actual passage of the Eighteenth Amendment, the idea that famously hard-drinking America would seriously attempt a liquor ban still seemed a bit far-fetched.

The collision of old and new sent the Reagans' stay in Chicago off to a slightly rocky start. One evening, not long after the family's arrival, Jack and Nelle went out for a rare evening on the town, leaving their two boys, ages four and six, home alone. Small children are not known for their accurate sense of the passage of time and, after a brief while, Moon and Dutch began to worry. It must have been Moon who decided they should go out looking for their parents. The youngsters carefully extinguished the lamps in their new apartment, assuming the flames they were blowing out must be connected to oil lamps, such as they were accustomed to using now and again back in Tampico. The lamps were actually gas jets.

Out onto the bustling Chicago sidewalk went Moon and Dutch. Since they were country kids who were comfortable, even at such a tender age, with roaming far and wide, there's no telling how far they might have gone were it not for a nearby tavern owner (or, in some accounts, an amiable inebriate) who spotted them wandering down the street. Reasoning that worried parents couldn't be far behind, he corralled the two youngsters. In the meantime, Jack and Nelle returned home to a flat full of gas fumes but conspicuously empty of children. Naturally, panic ensued. The boys were quickly located, though, and, as my father remembers it, "Jack clobbered us."

That, I strongly suspect, is a bit of hyperbole, a handy tagline of a sort often appended to stories about Jack when Dad penned his autobiographies. Whatever other faults may have been Jack's, there is no evidence that he physically abused his children. Moon, as the older brother and likely instigator of their foray onto the streets of Chicago, may well have received a spanking. Dutch, at age four, could hardly have been held responsible for this wanderlust and probably endured nothing more than a scolding. Hitting kids, I'm happy to report, simply doesn't seem to be in the Reagan DNA. It certainly wasn't part of my father's repertoire.

I will now share with you the one and only instance in which I witnessed Dad resorting to violent physical punishment with one of his children. I was perhaps six years old, which would have made it the summer of 1964. My father had taken me and my sister Patti to the family ranch in the Malibu hills, some 600 acres of horse pasture and rolling, oak-covered slopes north of Los Angeles, on one of our regular weekend outings. Patti, like many 12-year-old girls lucky enough to be presented with the opportunity, had become an avid equestrian after Dad had purchased a horse for her. I would often watch as he led her to a fenced ring behind our dilapidated house on the property to instruct her in the finer points of riding. True to family tradition, I eventually acquired my own steed as well, a cantankerous old packhorse named Popeye. Sullen and obstinate, he liked nothing better than to veer from trails into the brush in an effort to rub me off his back with the help of any convenient low-hanging tree limb. Try as I might — tugging the reins, kicking with my little cowboy-booted feet — there was nothing I could do to dissuade the malevolent and implacable Popeye. "Show him who's boss," my father would call out as my horse and I plunged into some manzanita-choked gully. I weighed perhaps 45 pounds; Popeye must have topped 1,000. It never occurred to me that the issue of who was in charge was really in question. With months of practice, I developed mediocre riding skills but impressive expertise when it came to dismounting while in motion. Popeye would try to dislodge me in his usual demonic fashion, and I would simply abandon ship, swinging a leg over the saddlehorn and sliding to the ground, thereby thwarting his plan to drag me to my doom. My father, I reasoned, though exasperated, seemed perfectly capable of rounding up my wayward mount.

I'm not sure exactly when the trouble started. The three of us — along with Lady, the family dog — were on our way back from the ranch that afternoon, my father at the wheel of our wood-paneled station wagon as we drove the winding Malibu Canyon Road toward the coast. We had traveled this route countless times in true early sixties' southern California fashion — hot afternoon sun beating through the windshield; no seat belts; and Dad with a can of cold Budweiser gripped between his thighs. With any luck, we'd stop for a frosty cone when we hit the Pacific Coast Highway. As usual, I was riding in the "way-back," the rear bay of the car where it was easier to take aim at passing motorists with my Davy Crockett long rifle. Patti and Dad had been arguing since we'd left the ranch about something beyond my six-year-old purview. Things were getting a bit heated, though — heated enough that I stopped drawing down on unwary drivers and slipped instead into the tingling, childish state of anticipation aroused by the prospect of seeing a sibling get into really big trouble.

Dad was already wearing his sternest expression — the sort he'd later assume as governor whenever addressing university students protesting the Vietnam War. And he was using his stern voice, too, the one that told you that the time for talking back was over. Dad never really raised his voice; instead, his tone would steadily acquire more gravity, until whatever complaining you might be doing began to sound, in your own ears, like the squeaking of gerbils. I knew things had grown especially tense when we didn't even take a break to yell out the window and make echoes as we passed through the big tunnel halfway through the canyon.

Let me stipulate here that Patti, aged 12, while a bright and funny girl, could be absolutely insufferable when she put her mind to it. Whatever she was going on about on this day, she had clearly given it her utmost consideration. By the tension in Dad's jaw and the whiteness of his knuckles flexing around the steering wheel, I could tell she was pushing him to about as near to a loss of temper as I'd yet seen.

It was just after we emerged from the darkness of the tunnel that my sister, responding to something (no doubt stern) my father had said, made her big mistake, complaining, "Jesus Christ, Dad!" In a blink, my father's right hand shot out, and he delivered what, from my present perspective as a sober, adult, child-advocate type, I would characterize as a light fingertip slap to Patti's left cheek. "Do not use the Lord's name in vain!" was all he said. Fifteen minutes or more of expert preteen goading, and he had mustered just enough rage for a gentle tap — and that only to stick up for Jesus.

The slap, which barely turned Patti's head, did no damage. But it earned Dad a withering glower from his daughter, and we rode the rest of the way home under a tearful, sulky cloud.

Whatever physical aggression my father and I might have felt toward each other was most likely diffused by the manly art of horsing around. Until embarrassingly well into my teens, I could be counted on to subject my father to a good-natured pugilistic battering without the slightest provocation — mostly jostling faux body blows, but he'd even tolerate the occasional tap to the cheek. By the time the poor man reached his sixties, I must have been driving him into a state of exhaustion. "I just want to know when he's going to get over this whole Oedipal complex thing," I once heard him tell my mother in slightly desperate tones. She had probably been counseling patience, reassuring him that I was just going through a phase — which I suppose I was.

I would soon learn that not everyone tolerates such games. And some people, I came to suspect, took exception to my clownish boxing with my father.

When Dad became governor of California, he was assigned drivers from the California Highway Patrol. His principal driver, Barney Barnett — as hearty and good-natured a fellow as ever walked the earth — would eventually become indispensable to our family, acting, among other things, as Dad's chief fence-building, brush-clearing buddy at the ranch my parents ultimately acquired north of Santa Barbara. The other officer — whom I'll call, with all due affection, Shemp, to avoid any potential lingering embarrassment — I mostly thought of as the guy who covered for Barney on his days off. Like a lot of CHP officers, Shemp was a big, strapping son of a gun — maybe six four, 220 pounds or so. We'd become quite familiar over the years, so one morning when I was around 13 or 14, I thought nothing of approaching Shemp as he waited for my father to leave the house and miming a few uppercuts to his midsection — as I might have my father, but without actually making any contact. Before I knew it, Shemp had locked my skinny wrist in a viselike grip and began bending me painfully toward the ground. There was nothing playful in his gesture, and for a moment I truly thought he might snap some bones. After what seemed like an unnecessarily long time to make whatever point he had in mind, Shemp released me and warned, "Don't ever raise your hands to a man unless you really mean to use them." He was staring at me stone-faced, without a trace of humor or goodwill. In retrospect, I think Shemp may have taken exception to my roughhousing with my father and decided to put me in my place — a timely lesson from the sort of guy who probably never won any parenting awards.

I never told either of my parents about this incident. I had internalized the common kid ethic, which prohibited ratting people out over matters like that. If I had a beef with Shemp, then I'd have to take it up with him on my own. Since that was unlikely to be productive, it was better to let the matter drop. Besides, if it came to a dispute between Shemp and me, I wasn't entirely sure whose side my parents would take. Both had the deep, almost automatic respect for authority figures common to their generation. Shemp's behavior might have been way over the top, but he wore a uniform and a badge.

He was, nominally, a grown-up and, what's more, one sworn to "serve and protect." I, on the other hand, a mere kid, had been known to make trouble. My hair had grown disturbingly long and my clothing, much of it picked up in thrift stores, no longer fit the "good boy" category. Over the preceding couple of years I had declared myself an atheist and let it be known that I didn't support the Vietnam War. It was becoming obvious that I was a poor candidate for membership in the Young Republicans. Given my track record, I could too easily imagine my father lending Shemp a sympathetic ear, for such a situation created an unfortunate mash-up between two of his notable weaknesses: his almost pathological squeamishness with regard to interpersonal conflict and his reflexive tendency to defer to perceived experts. As his child, you learned to pick the fights you could win.

My elder brother and sister seem to have felt similar misgivings under far more trying circumstances. Michael, as he has revealed in his memoirs, was sexually abused as a young boy by a summer camp counselor. There are many reasons why a child might keep such a trauma to himself, but it is notable that Michael never once sought his father's help. During her first marriage,

Maureen was routinely brutalized by her husband, a policeman. Yet she, too, never brought this to Dad's attention.

I think Michael and Maureen simply had him wrong. Certainly he would have gone berserk on anybody who'd molested his son. In Maureen's situation, too, I have a hard time imagining him — had he known — failing to intervene. He could be oblivious, but he was not uncaring.

Despite his growing dismay at my budding counterculture sensibilities, only once in my life did I think that my father might actually take a swing at me. I was 17, maybe 18. My days under my parents' roof, I knew, were numbered. Unlike many in the current crop of parents, mine didn't regard their kids as having much of a right to privacy as long as they were living in the family home. Evidence of their visits to my room while I was out and telltale clicking on the phone line convinced me that if I wanted any space to myself, I would have to find it elsewhere. I don't recall what we were fighting about on the night in question, but, as was often the case, the decisive battle was being waged at the dinner table. My father often frustrated my mother by conveniently checking out of dinnertime confrontations. Mom and I would be going back and forth with increasing acrimony about one thing or another while, at the other end of the table, Dad kept his head down, busily spearing charred bits of roast beef tip or hiding his uneaten vegetables under lumps of mashed potatoes. "Honey!" Mom would snap, finally setting her fork down with a crack like a rifle shot and shooting a look across the table at her seemingly oblivious husband. Oh, how he must have hated those moments, being dragged into the middle of some messy, often pointless dispute, forced to weather the tempests of teenage misery. He was always acutely uncomfortable with roiling emotion and harsh words. He must have realized, with grim resignation born of experience, that there was no way to emerge from such altercations unblemished. Nobody can muddy a hero's cape as casually as an insolent teenager.

This night, though, Dad had been prepped and girded for battle: This was meant to be a full-contact, two-on-one confrontation, with my mother and him working in concert. We went around and around for a while, the three of us, bobbing and weaving, admonishing and recriminating, until, outnumbered and harried, I attempted a tactical retreat. "This is getting us nowhere," I said, folding my napkin on the table. "I'm going out for a drive." "You're not going anywhere, Mister," my father replied (need I add, in his stern voice). That posed what amounted to an irresistible challenge to my youthful sense of autonomy and, sliding my chair back, I stood up and blithely said, "Bye!" When I was about halfway across the living room, I heard his voice behind me, "You come back here and sit down, right now!" I kept walking, but as I reached the front door I heard him push back from the table (in my memory, his chair topples over) and start after me. Turning toward him with one hand gripping the doorknob, I watched as he strode across the gray shag carpet, the hem of his bathrobe flapping as he moved. Something about that flapping robe — perhaps its slightly absurd air of femininity — made me feel, even in that moment, a kind of tender sympathy for him. "Hold it right there!" he barked. More than anything, it was my open defiance that had angered him; he might no longer have remembered, much less cared, what we were originally fighting about. It was the midseventies, and by then he'd had about as much as he could take of shaggy-haired, ungrateful kids flipping off those he considered to be responsible parental figures. *That* wasn't going to happen under his roof.

117

As he arrived at the slate floor of the entry hall, I was semidetachedly wondering how all this would play out. My musing ceased, however, when I saw him cock his right fist. Even in his midsixties, my father gave the impression that he was decidedly not the sort of guy with whom you'd want to mix it up. This impression was all the more effective because he never blustered. I never heard my father growl about kicking someone's ass, certainly never saw him actually threaten anyone. He was a pretty big guy, of course, but it wasn't his size so much as it was merely something about the way he held himself in certain moments that said "I don't want to knock you ass over teakettle, so if I do, you'll know you really deserved it." Dad and his clenched fist were now a only couple of steps away. Without really considering what I was doing, I took a half step toward him and, in a purely defensive gesture meant to arrest his charge, shot out my left hand, catching him flush in the sternum with the flat of my palm. With his momentum brought to a halt, his slipper-shod feet came out from under him on the slick floor and he stumbled backward. Taking advantage of the reprieve, I quickly swung out of the door, glancing back for just a split second to see him steadying himself, a look of utter surprise falling across his face.

This was not, to say the least, the way I preferred to conclude any interaction with my father, no matter how angry. Resolving to try to set things right, I waited a couple of days until tempers had cooled, and then approached my mother and explained my feelings about the matter of potential fisti-cuffs between my father and me. By now the topic of the original dispute had faded to insignificance in light of this new escalation of father/son tension. My mother, always more concerned with pacifying family rela-tions than with the details of any particular argument, backed me up. The next time the three of us were together, I broached the subject. "Dad, I hope you know that I would never hit you. But I don't want you hitting me, either. So why don't we agree be-tween us that, whatever else happens, we're not going to raise our hands against each other?" My mother had thoroughly briefed him in advance, of course. But I could sense his gratitude that this potentially ugly busi-ness could be safely edited from our family lore. We shook hands on it, and the incident — never again referred to by either party — became the first and last time there was any threat of an actual physical altercation between us.

■■■■

I digress. The Reagans remained in Chicago only long enough for my father to register one more genuine memory. One night he and Moon were awakened by a loud commotion. Rushing to their second-story apartment's front window, they watched as a fire wagon drawn by a team of horses clanged and thundered past below them.

That summer, Jack was arrested for public drunkenness. Details of the incident are unknown, but it resulted in his losing his new job at the Fair Department Store. The Reagan family packed up for another move, away from the bright promise of cosmopolitan life and back to the confines of a small town surrounded by tall corn. Little Dutch would have known nothing of his father's fall from grace. Nelle, on the other hand, must have been furious, and her anger no doubt cast a pall over the retreating family. But perhaps she experienced a rush of relief as well: happy to be leaving such a whiskey-soaked metropolis and eager to return to a smaller stage, one she could more easily manage and from which she could better keep her eye on Jack. Her selection of Galesburg, nearly 150 miles west-southwest of their flat on Chicago's South Side

120

and redolent with the effluvia of its thriving market for horses and mules, may have had something to do with that town's early embrace of temperance.

Jack took a job selling shoes at a large store downtown. The family moved first to temporary quarters in a small bungalow, then to a larger house they rented on North Kellogg Street, walking distance from Jack's new place of employment. Moon was enrolled in first grade at the Silas Willard School. Dutch, not yet five, stayed home; there was no such thing as public school kindergarten in those days.

He received something of an education nonetheless. Nelle was in the habit of settling in between her two sons as she put them to bed and reading to them aloud, her finger tracking with her voice, word to word, line after line. Eventually, almost unconsciously and prior to any formal instruction, my father learned to decipher print on a page.

One evening in the summer of 1916, Jack returned home from fitting shoes to find his younger son sprawled on the floor of their parlor with a copy of the *Galesburg Evening Mail* spread out before him. "What are you doing?" he asked. "Reading," came the offhand reply. Suspecting that his boy was having a bit of fun with him, Jack accepted the challenge. "Yeah? Read me something, then!" Without hesitation Dutch complied. Jack was astounded; his son was some sort of prodigy. Nelle was alerted to the wonder in their midst, and out they went to round up as many neighbors as they could find. Soon an audience had gathered around Dutch, and they all listened, duly impressed, as he read them a headline about a "powder blast" on Black Tom Island.

It is during his stay in Galesburg that we begin to sense the emerging lineaments of my father's personality. He was deeply attracted to his new town's dark red-brick paving and the maples that thickly clustered along its streets. They fitted into a "picture of bright-colored peace," he would later remember. This peace may have held a hopeful attraction for him, given Jack's continued drinking and the fractiousness it introduced to the home front. It was around this time, too, that he became acutely conscious of it as a source of tension between his parents. He would feign sleep at night as the voices from their room rose in volume — Nelle laying into Jack for his binging, Jack, in his caustic way, giving as good as he got. It is tempting to suppose that Dad's avoidance of interpersonal conflict later in life stemmed from these anxious nights spent curled under his bedcovers, trying to drown out the angry altercations with a more soothing refrain only he could hear. It may have been during these moments, as well, that he began developing his preternatural talent for excising unpleasantness from his picture of reality — or replacing that reality altogether with a more uplifting version concocted in his head.

His newfound talent for reading afforded him some solace. At the same time, his extreme nearsightedness, which would go unrecognized until he was older, would render the wider world a smudgy blur, impelled him toward a close and solitary examination of the natural world.

The Galesburg house had an attic in which the landlord had left a hodgepodge of various artifacts. This dimly lit space beneath the roof beams, to which no one else in the family seemed drawn, provided my father, perhaps for the first time, with an opportunity to take refuge from the world in a place of stillness and silence, where his imagination could take flight. "Here, I ran across a forgotten, enormous collection of bird's eggs and butterflies. . . . They became gateways to the mysterious, symbols of the out-of-doors they represented. Here, in the musty attic dust, I got my first scent of wind on peaks, pine needles in the rain, and visions of sunrise on the desert." That's packing a lot into a trove of desiccated eggshells and insects.

All that time spent alone focusing on nature's detritus also seems to have had a salutary effect on his ability to concentrate. In 1917, when he registered for first grade, joining Moon at the Willard School, he immediately became a standout student, earning straight As. Dad always claimed — without making much of a fuss about it — that, at least as a child, he was blessed with a photographic memory. That may well have been the case; he seems to have had little trouble memorizing spelling words and, as he progressed through school, multiplication tables and historical dates.

While the Reagans were in Galesburg, America entered World War I. Dad was under the impression that Jack was first in line to enlist, only to be turned away because the army wasn't taking fathers with two or more children. Jack, Dad later wrote, rued being born between war generations — too young for the Spanish-American War; too old for World War I. Perhaps. Whether willingly or not, he was part of a long Reagan family pattern of missing combat, a tradition

Dad would continue — also regretfully — when World War II broke out.

Maybe Jack was looking forward to decamping to a country with a more tolerant attitude toward liquor consumption. In Galesburg he seems to have gotten himself into his usual trouble, requiring the usual resort to new employment. Down the road, a few miles west to the tiny village of Monmouth, went the Reagans, Jack having secured yet another job selling shoes.

Young Dutch was enrolled at Monmouth's Central School, and there, too, immediately impressed teachers with his ability to memorize and recall facts and figures, so much so that he was promoted ahead of his classmates into the third grade. This, together with his small size and distracted demeanor, did not endear him to the neighborhood bullies, who took to hounding him on his way home from school. But he would soon be reminded that his solitude could be breached in more consequential ways.

In October of that year the Spanish flu came to Monmouth along with a trainload of apples from New York State. On the thirteenth of the month, the local health officer declared an emergency and closed schools, churches, libraries, and any other place where people might congregate in numbers.

The worst pandemic in recorded history had arrived at the Reagan family's doorstep.

I had a little bird,
Its name was Enza.
I opened the window,
And in-flu-enza.

Children skipped rope to that rhyme in the fall of 1918. The slaughter in Europe was nearly over, but a chance rearrangement of proteins on the surface of an otherwise common virus had created a monster already on its way to killing 20 million to 50 million people worldwide — more than had been lost in four years of trench fighting during "the war to end all wars"; more people, in fact, than had perished during the years of the fourteenth-century Black Death. The virus would be contracted by 28 percent of Americans; an estimated 675,000 would die from it. One oddity of the infection: Unlike typical influenza, which generally takes its highest toll among the very old and very young, this variant proved especially deadly to adults aged 20 to 40.

Nelle fell ill. That she survived the first hours was a hopeful sign, for the afflicted were known to succumb within the course of a day. One story making the rounds that autumn had four women sitting down for an evening's bridge game; by morning, three were dead. Many victims rapidly developed an especially viscous pneumonia and then, as one physician put it, "died struggling to clear their airways of a blood-tinged froth that sometimes gushed from their nose and mouth." Medical science of the day was helpless before the onslaught. There was nothing Nelle's doctor could do for her. Jack, who ordinarily attended mass on an intermittent basis, began lighting candles daily at the altar. The boys hovered anxiously, waiting for the doctor to pronounce the end. Instead, in desperation, he advised the family to feed her as much moldy cheese as she could stomach. There is no medical reason that a virus would respond to what the doctor may have supposed was a crude form of antibiotic. But Nelle recovered nonetheless, her indomitable will refusing to submit to a mere pathogen. For the rest of his life, my father would credit the cheese.

There followed, in the small hours of November 11, a great and raucous celebration: Armistice Day. The war was over, and with it the last exhalation of the nineteenth century. The twentieth century was now fully underway, with America leading the parade as the world's preeminent industrial power. From now on, the velocity of change would seem to increase exponentially almost year to year. To cite one small but telling example: In the decade after World War I, women's fashion changed more radically than at any time in history, before or since. Bustles, corsets, and bows, all the lacy, elaborate filigree of the Victorian era, not to mention piles of long locks in intricate, fastidiously pinned swirls, would be thrown aside — at least among the younger generations in more fashion-forward circles — for a drastically simplified mode of dress and short bobbed hair that, in many cases, looks entirely modern to this day. More importantly, in 1920 women would gain the right to vote — an overdue change Nelle certainly approved of.

All this concentrated upheaval at a tender age does not seem to have sat easily with Dutch. Even the armistice was a disturbing intrusion. "The parades, the torches, the bands, the shoutings [sic] and drunks, and the burning of Kaiser Bill in effigy," he would later write, "created in me an uneasy feeling of a world outside my own." That world, or at least parts of it, would one day exert a powerful fascination, but for now Dutch Reagan was happiest in a small place with familiar contours, bounded on all sides by the dry rustling of cornstalks and still governed by customs tied to the round of the seasons. School photos from the time show a little fellow who has developed a habitual nervous gesture, his left hand seeming to tug at nonexistent chin whiskers. The beaming energy of his infant portraits appears, by his early boyhood, to have turned inward.

There was one more stop to make before the Reagan family reached a place where they could put down real roots. In the fall of 1919, they returned for just over a year to my father's birthplace, Tampico. Jack once more went to work for H. C. Pitney, this time as manager of his dry goods emporium. The family moved into an apartment directly above the store. My father remembers this time as a rustic interlude, an idyll of woods and fields, creek and canal. (The photo hanging in his birthplace dates from this period.) Schoolwork posed few challenges for him. Jack had taken to spending time on the road. Moon was running with a gang of bigger boys. Nelle, true to form, was assuming a leadership role in her church, the Tampico branch of which was, for the time being, shy a preacher. Though not without friends, young Dutch took to spending much of his time on his own, free to wander the landscape beyond the tiny grid of streets. This seemed to suit him. Here was a chance to begin cultivating his solitary inner self.

During this interlude he was more or less adopted by an elderly couple living next door, a jeweler and his wife whom Dutch came to think of as Uncle Jim and Aunt Emma. They gave him an allowance of $0.10 per week and cookies and chocolate every afternoon when school let out. "The best part was that I was allowed to dream," he remembered. The jeweler's shop and the couple's apartment above it were virtually stagecrafted to delight such a pensive youngster. He would later recall "the mystic atmosphere of Aunt Emma's living room with its horsehair-stuffed gargoyles of furniture, its shawls and antimacassars, globes of glass over birds and flowers, books and strange odors." This kindly pair, who had no children of their own, seem to have intuited and graciously accepted this slightly odd little neighbor boy's need to simply be left alone. They provided him something he would come to seek throughout his life: a safe sanctuary in which to nurture his private thoughts.

All this would have long since become irrelevant, needless to say, had a new friend, Monkey Winchell, succeeded, quite unintentionally no doubt, in killing my father. Monkey was so called on account of his easily piqued curiosity — and because, apparently, during this era no one was ever referred to by his given name. Something that particularly fascinated Monkey was his father's pump-action shotgun. One Saturday night, while their parents were downstairs, the two boys crept into Monkey's parents' bedroom and retrieved the weapon. Monkey aimed the barrel toward the ceiling and squeezed the trigger to no effect. My father, not to be outdone, grabbed the gun, pumped it, and did the same. An ear-bursting blast was accompanied by a strong whiff of gunpowder, mingling with the dust of falling plaster. When their frantic parents reached them they found both boys sitting quietly under a considerable hole in the Winchells' ceiling, pretending to be engrossed in issues of the *Sunday School Quarterly*.

So here stands our hero, aged nine, hand thoughtfully tugging at his chin, straight brow slightly furrowed, peering into a middle distance he can barely discern and from which, he expects, unpleasant things may emerge. What sort of child do we have before us? What dreams unspool behind his nearsighted eyes? His earliest years suggest a baseline joie de vivre. He is bright, has an unusually keen memory, and might even be considered bookish but with a taste mostly for fantasy and adventure. Unlike his older brother, he gives his mother little trouble. He is a good boy. Given the somewhat chaotic circumstances of his upbringing, it's not surprising that he craves order and predictability. He is comfortable in the company of others but seems utterly content — perhaps most content — to be alone, free to follow his thoughts without interruption. Though full of energy, he is small for his age and, among his peers, is often picked last for games on the playfield. This, along with his family's years of wandering — which have left him the perennial new kid at a succession of schools — has contributed to a sense of insecurity now heightened by a growing awareness that all is not entirely well between his parents. Nevertheless, aside from occasional experiences of claustrophobia — at the bottom of kid pileups he feels a suffocating terror — he is physically fearless; the sluggish brown waters of nearby canals, the fields spreading toward the horizon on all sides with their grass snakes and toads hold few terrors for him. It is what he can't see or what jarringly, if fleetingly, intrudes from the world beyond that causes him worry. He is already creating in his mind a patchwork account of life and his place in it. Naturally he is at the center of this tale — looming so large, in fact, that other people are sometimes reduced to props or bit players. He will go on refining this story throughout his life, in the process becoming not just its creator and star but director and story editor as well. Eventually that story will be buffed to a lustrous sheen, its rough spots worn smooth in the retelling, his own role ripened into one of unassailable nobility. As years pass he will, in effect, become his story. But for now, he is just a small boy living in rented rooms above a little shop in one of countless farm towns dotting a landscape he is barely beginning to fathom.

Jack, meanwhile, approaching his late thirties, is still looking to establish himself as something more than a dry goods clerk. He realizes that his prospects in Tampico are inherently limited. He needs a new venue, one that will draw a more moneyed clientele, people of cosmopolitan taste who will appreciate the services he is so well prepared to offer. And it wouldn't hurt to have a profit-sharing stake in the business. By the fall of 1920 he has convinced H. C. Pitney to close the store in Tampico and transfer their budding partnership about 20 miles northwest to a larger, industry-based town on the banks of the Rock River. This town, Dixon, more than any other the Reagans have lived in, will come to mean home to my father. It will serve as his original template for the "shining city" he will later extol as a model for all that is good in American life.

CHAPTER FIVE
DIXON

Turning west off the 294 onto Interstate 88, I swing onto the Ronald Reagan Memorial Tollway and begin to enter the heart of Reagan Country. Not the Reagan Country of political ads, the "Morning in America" Reagan Country, with its Old Glory bunting, soft focus, stiff hairdos. This is the real deal: rail lines, truck stops, farm fields cut by streams and canals. I watch genuine family history slide past the windows of my mid-size rent-a-bucket. This is approximately the route my great-great-grandparents would have taken over 150 years ago as they rode the train from Chicago heading for their new homestead on the prairie around Fairhaven Township. The wind turbines now rotating majestically in a freshening west wind, not to mention the sheer number of businesses offering fried food to the hungry traveler, would have astonished them, but the road signs announcing Aurora, DeKalb,

Rochelle, and Malta would be familiar — familiar, as well, to Dutch Reagan from earliest boyhood.

Still, the tollway is incongruous. My father would hardly object to having a highway named after him and would likely express modest, aw-shucks gratitude for a bridge or even a tunnel. But a tollway? I'm pretty sure he'd have reservations. Out west, when I was growing up, nobody paid tolls to get around; that was a behavioral oddity of plainly confused Easterners. We had freeways — *freeways* (except for the Golden Gate Bridge, which was, after all, a tourist attraction and could be thought of as offering visitors from parts east a welcoming touch of home). This may be surprising, since Dad had a reputation for callousness when it came to the poor, but I think he would find the idea of dropping $1.90 into someone's hand every few miles for the pleasure of a less crowded commute inherently unfair, even undemocratic. Having to constantly slow down or stop would also annoy him.

I'll have to get used to such incongruities, I figure, now that I'm on the Ronald Reagan Trail, a tourist-friendly path laid out in various brochures and advertised online. Another Illinoisan former president, Abraham Lincoln, gets his due hereabouts, but in the quest for the dollars rolling in on the bus tours these days, Ronald Reagan appears to be the headliner. There are helpful road maps to all the key landmarks of his early life, from his birthplace in Tampico to his alma mater, Eureka College — even, if you care to cross the state line, to radio stations WOC and WHO in Davenport and Des Moines, Iowa. But one venue claims pride of place.

Ahead, beneath a lowering pewter sky already spitting fat raindrops, is the city of Dixon, crown jewel of the trail.

Sometime during the warm months of 1828, a fellow of mixed French and Native American ancestry named Joseph Ogee built himself a cabin near the Rock River just south of the Grand Detour, a pronounced oxbow in the river, the banks of which were lined with stands of black walnut, oak, wild plum, and thorn apple. It was extravagantly lush country. Rushing around several islands thick with willow, the water ran clear over a bed of sand and stones. Abundant deer wandered through meadow and forest. Aboriginal legend had it — so the story goes — that the river, reluctant to depart the bountiful lands it had just passed through, turned back here for one last, lingering look before setting a straighter southwest course on its way to merging with the Mississippi.

When Ogee arrived, this sylvan mix of woodland and prairie was still the province of the Illini and Dakota Sioux. The discovery of rich veins of lead to the northwest at Galena was already hastening the end of their dominion. Europeans drawn west by the prospect of mineral wealth would need to cross the Rock River, however, and Ogee provided the ferry. But by the spring of 1830, either motivated by wanderlust or worn out by recalcitrant natives setting fire to his dock, he decided to pull up stakes and sold his thriving river shuttle to John Dixon, who promptly christened the spot — and who could fault him? — Dixon's Ferry.

On July 10 of that year a Sauk chief named Keokuk cut a deal with the invaders, selling 26.5 million acres of land east of the Mississippi to the U.S. government for the bargain price of $0.03 per acre. Included in the sale was a village at the junction of the Rock and the Mississippi rivers that had been occupied by members of the Sauk and Fox tribes for over 150 years, ever since they were driven by the French from their ancestral homes on the Michigan peninsula. This village happened to be the home of Black Hawk, war chief of the Sauk and Fox. Returning home in early fall from a hunting trip, he was startled and outraged to find his village occupied by white settlers, and he made threatening noises about driving them out. The settlers, terrified, appealed to Illinois governor John Reynolds, who, in response, called up a volunteer militia. Suddenly outnumbered and ill prepared for large-scale conflict, Black Hawk retreated with his band to the western shores of the Mississippi, there to strategize his return.

Two years later, on April 6, 1832, Black Hawk and 1,000 of his followers crossed back into Illinois in an attempt to reclaim their territory.

The federal government ultimately dispatched General Winfield Scott to solve the predicament of an indigenous people's objecting to being driven from their land. (Of note to presidential historians: Among the eager militiamen billeted together in Fort Dixon's Nachusa House hotel during the conflict were not only Captain Abraham Lincoln of the Sangamon County volunteers, but his superior officer, Lieutenant Jefferson Davis, future leader of the Confederacy.) Scott's men spent the month of July chasing Black Hawk to and fro across the Northern Illinois prairie. Finally, on August 1, near the confluence of the Bad Axe and Mississippi rivers in Wisconsin, with his people exhausted and starving, Black Hawk surrendered. Violence broke out anew, however, when troops tried to lock him up aboard a ship anchored in the river. Hundreds of his people, who had already crossed the Mississippi back to "their" shore, were gunned down. Black Hawk escaped with a small group, including 35 women and children, but his days as a free man were numbered. He was captured for the final time four weeks later. His defeat would mark the end of organized Native American resistance to white settlement in Northern Illinois.

Growing up, I knew nothing of the campaign that would come to be known as the Black Hawk War. But when it came to games of cowboys and Indians, I, like many little kids, had a decided preference for the natives. Perhaps because that's what they were: the home team. Even in the absurdly revisionist movies and TV shows of my childhood — *Daniel Boone* and *The Lone Ranger* — it was clear that the land belonged to the Sioux, Comanche, Cherokee, or whomever because they belonged to the land. No matter how skewed its entertainments were to the paleface perspective, Hollywood could never quite disguise, even in cheap fiction with nonnative actors, the uncomfortable reality that these "savages" were actually the rightful occupiers of the territory that we, with our cavalry and our cattle, our steam trains, six-shooters, and saloons, were determined to take — by brute force, if the locals had the temerity to resist.

"But they were here for, like, thousands of years before we came. What gave us the right to take their home away?" It was my first awakening to social injustice — the seed, after an indeterminate gestation, suddenly sprouting with the appearance of an Indian character on TV. Dad was bearing the brunt of it. That's the way it was in our house: For any practical, day-to-day issues — hunger, out of underwear, bleeding profusely — you went to my mother. My father was on call for the big questions — like, How come, if Jesus says we're supposed to treat everyone the way we'd want to be treated, we're stealing these people's ancestral grounds? I could be a terrier on issues like this, and for this particular one I was determined not to let him off the hook. He'd first tried to tell me that there weren't really very many Indians around to begin with, so it was nothing to get worked up about. I countered that they seemed to be sufficiently numerous that the cavalry was required to displace them (not my exact words at age 9 or 10, but that was the gist). Dad then insisted that the land had been going to waste; the Indians weren't properly exploiting its natural bounty. I could hear the pitch of my voice begin to rise as I objected. It was their land! If I noticed that you hadn't bothered to install a pool in your backyard, did that mean I could take your house? "Well . . ." the arrows were flying thick and fast, and Dad was running out of bullets. "The thing is," he finally offered, exasperated, "the Indians just didn't understand the concept of private property."

His tone suggested this would be his last word on the subject, at least until he'd had time to formulate a better argument. I knew if I persisted he would turn to his default response in our arguments and accuse me of being a "locker room lawyer," meaning I was resorting to unworthy semantic tactics and becoming a "pain in the keister." This may not have been the first time I had pushed him into what I saw as an untenable position, but it gave me a squirmingly uncomfortable feeling nonetheless. I could accept that there was a historical explanation for white Europeans overrunning North America. But the moral and ethical justification for this land grab was not apparent, and my father's arguments to the contrary were unpersuasive. Bothered as I was by the plight of my war-painted playtime avatars, I was even more confused by Dad's taking the side of the bad guys — even if the bad guys were us. Why couldn't he admit that Americans had done a bad thing? I just wanted an obvious injustice acknowledged. Little did I suspect at that age what damage such an admission might do to his cherished notions of America's divine providence. But it was clear even then that he was struggling with something far more significant than a need to win an argument with his child. "I can't help feeling that the Lord put America here between two oceans for a purpose," he used to say with a kind of unblinking innocence. Observing that Africa, South America, Australia, and, while we're at it, the entire Eurasian landmass are "between two oceans" as well left you feeling like you'd taken a wrecking ball to his idea of the nation as a spotless, peerless "shining city." There were some things about our country, its past, and, come to think of it, life in general that Dad's internal construct of the world was not built to encompass, and I took it upon myself at a fairly early age to confront him with them (at least as I understood them). Maybe I just enjoyed tormenting him. But it seemed, somehow, necessary.

At that point, mercifully, the commercial

break ended, and we went back to watching Fess Parker in a coonskin cap wandering the Santa Monica Mountains as Kentuckian Daniel Boone — crucially assisted, as usual, by Ed Ames in the role of his Native American sidekick, Mingo.

Referring to the land he had lost surrounding the Grand Detour, Black Hawk told his captors, "The Rock River was a beautiful country. I loved it and I fought for it. It is now yours. Keep it as we did."

That was, of course, wishful thinking. By 1845 the population of Dixon had grown from a few scattered families to 400. The first of several dams was soon constructed across the Rock. Mills of various types followed, taking advantage of the river's power. During the area's cold winters, the river could freeze to a depth of 16 inches. Teams of horses would be employed to remove snow and plane smooth the surface of the ice, which would then be cut into manageable blocks and stored between layers of sawdust or hay in icehouses built along the river's east bank. In 1905 the Dixon Pure Ice Company was employing over 50 men and exporting some 15,000 tons of ice by rail. Dixon never became a one-industry town, however, and its diversity enabled it to thrive modestly despite the economic ups and downs of the late nineteenth century.

By the time of the Reagan family's arrival in early December of 1920 — and with the town's population having grown to around 10,000, nearly 10 times that of Tampico — Dixon had reached a respectable, self-satisfied middle age. Granted, it was not destined to take its place alongside cities the size of Aurora or DeKalb, but its embrace of the Rock River — and the river's Mississippi-bound traffic — would always make it indispensable. With his brief stay in Chicago little more than a dim and distant memory, nine-year-old Dutch Reagan must have viewed his new home as quite a metropolis.

EXCLUSIVENESS
QUALITY STYLE

The Characteristics of
Eastern Shoe Making are
Strongly Emphasized in
"Our Shoes for People of Fashion"

Standing in the third-floor hallway of my father's old middle school, now the Dixon Historic Center, looking through a glass display window at this advertisement from Jack Reagan's pride and joy, I can't help but be impressed by its buoyant optimism. Jack was finally running the upscale enterprise of his dreams.

The February 28, 1921, edition of the *Dixon Telegraph* carried the news:

> H.C. Pitney and J.E. Reagan will open an exclusive shoe store in this city in the building formerly occupied by O.H. Brown & Co. All new fixtures have been installed, and the store will be stocked with all new spring styles. The new establishment will be known as the "Fashion Boot Shop." Mr. Reagan, who will act as manager, is an experienced shoe man and also a graduate practipedist and understands all foot troubles and the correct methods of relief for all foot discomforts, having had years of experience in this line in many of the larger cities throughout the state.

Well, maybe two of the "larger cities" — if you count Galesburg. But what's a little résumé padding when things finally seem to be turning around? As the new decade began the Reagan family was in a hopeful mood. Jack was sober and employed. Nelle was channeling her theatrical energy into religion, becoming active among the local Disciples of Christ. Moon would waste little time finding a new set of juvenile rowdies with whom to run among the working-class Irish on the town's south side. And to young Dutch, even with his smudgy nearsightedness, Dixon must have appeared tailor-made.

Within a short walk of their rented home was almost everything that would become the center of my father's life over the next few years. School was only four blocks north, toward the river; the public library where he would spend many afternoons lost in reverie was on the next corner; Nelle's First Christian Church was just one block farther still. Even the YMCA, where he would first be recognized as an unusually talented swimmer, was within easy strolling distance.

The house itself — a tidy, two-story, three-bedroom affair at 816 South Hennepin Avenue — was built in 1891 with a loan of $1,500 on land originally held by "Father" John Dixon. In 1917 it was purchased by a widow, Emma Donovan, for $3,000, then promptly resold to her son John and his wife, Theresa, at a $500 profit. They, in turn, rented it to the Reagans.

With its clapboards, shingles, and covered front porch, the Ronald Reagan Boyhood Home sits unobtrusively among its neighbors on a quiet, oak-sheltered street one block west of Dixon's main thoroughfare,

147

Galena Avenue — that is, until you spot the sign designating it a historical landmark and then let your eye wander over to the life-size bronze Ronald Reagan statue standing in the middle of the lot immediately to the south.

As in Tampico, I've decided not to announce my arrival in advance. My brother, Michael, had paid his first visit to Dixon only three months earlier. Photos of him arriving by bus with camera crew in tow, surrounded by local press and greeting locals, convinced me that that was not the optimal way to soak in the ambience of Dad's former stomping grounds. My anonymity vanishes, however, as soon as I cross the threshold of the Visitor Center next door to the home and hear, "It is him!" I immediately step into a warm shower of Reaganophilia.

I shouldn't have been surprised. That morning I'd pulled into a Dixon diner for breakfast. The place was packed; I took the only table open, a booth by the side window. Keeping my head down, I spread out my newspaper and did my best to assume an air of inconspicuousness. A couple of eggs with bacon later, I felt rather pleased with myself. As far as I could tell, I appeared to have flown under the local radar — no fevered whispering from fellow diners followed by

148

surreptitious glances. I signaled for the check, and a cheerful waitress approached. "Can I ask you something?" she eyed me curiously. "Umm, sure," I said, taking a quick look around, but nobody seemed to be paying attention; all were calmly engrossed in their coffee and waffles. "Everybody here is saying you're Ronald Reagan's son. Is that true?" After confirming her customers' suspicions, I paid up, and, trying not to feel like a self-conscious fool, made my way to the door amid a room full of folks doing their polite best not to stare.

Standing on the boyhood home's front porch with its executive director, Connie Lange, I marvel at what an ideal neighborhood it seems in which to pass a boyhood. The surrounding houses appear solidly middle class, fronted by large lawns suitable for games and thickly populated by spreading shade trees with climbable limbs. It is by now established lore regarding Dutch Reagan's early years that he grew up in a state not far removed from poverty. Without ever explicitly making such a claim, Dad nevertheless furthered that impression by highlighting his father's lost jobs, his mother's creative leftover stews, and his own need to work during his summers home from school. In truth, though Jack occasionally found himself searching for employment and the family rarely amassed much in the way of savings, the Reagans never counted themselves among the poor. They were never able to buy their own home, but the houses they rented (Jack and Nelle would, in the course of a 15-year stay, live in five different ones in Dixon) were reasonably spacious and comfortable. The impression I get — even visiting the Tampico apartment — is that while, during the early twentieth century, people of middling means like my grandparents lived with more scarcity than we do, they simultaneously enjoyed a different sort of abundance. True, there was no opportunity to choose among dozens of flat-screen televisions or discover which artificially scented push-button bathroom deodorizer best fit your personality; children's rooms weren't stuffed to the rafters with every conceivable robotic wonder toy. A profusion of media intake valves weren't constantly vacuuming you into the commercial multiverse; shopping was less a hobby than something you did when you truly needed something — and it required that you actually go somewhere and hand over real cash. You had a lot less stuff. But, if my father's circumstances were typical, you had space around you and more time to relax. With a regular job and a bit of luck, you could find a pretty decent place to live.

The Hennepin residence sits on a large rectangular lot near the crest of the avenue. It is flanked on its north side by the house that now serves as its visitor center and on its south by a small park with the requisite Reagan statue. Restoration work began in earnest after the property was turned over to the city in 1980. In what amounted to an exercise in urban archaeology, volunteers stripped the home to the studs and painstakingly restored its 1920s appearance. Additions were removed, floorboards replaced, fresh plaster applied, and a new roof put on. In the front room, five layers of wallpaper were peeled back, revealing a floral print, which Moon Reagan, acting as a part-time consultant on the project, thought he remembered from his boyhood. A wallpaper company was then commissioned to re-create a sufficient quantity to cover the parlor walls. Modern appliances were moved out; a twenties-style kitchen was installed. Period furniture was obtained and, once again, Moon offered advice on its placement. Virtually the only item remaining from the period of the Reagan family's occupation is the freestanding claw-foot bathtub; none of the workforce could cope with humping it down the narrow staircase from the sole bathroom on the second floor.

Throw in some modern conveniences, maybe add a bathroom, and in the Seattle neighborhood where my wife and I now live, Dad's old house would sell for over $500,000. I'm stunned when Connie guesses that a typical house on the block would go for $60,000 today. "Maybe $100,000, if it's one of the bigger ones."

The restoration is impressive, but as is usually the case when a previous era is studiously re-created, a trifle antiseptic. The Morris chair and other furniture jibe with my father and uncle's adult memories; the dishes set out in the dining room may be of the very pattern Nelle used. The popcorn bowl on a coffee table in the front parlor gets it right — the Reagans were big popcorn lovers. Still, one can't quite erase the knowledge that almost nothing here actually belonged to my family. I wonder whether airspace itself can retain remnants of the past.

Oddly — perhaps because its spartan decor seems least contrived — I find the boys' bedroom, in the northeast corner upstairs, the most compelling spot inside the house. A few football banners have been tacked to the wall to add some atmosphere. Beyond these, the room contains nothing but a single iron-framed bed facing a small dresser. Moon and Dutch, two strong, distinct personalities, each willful in his own way, during all their years living under the same roof somehow managed to share a mattress.

I've been wondering about Moon. Two and a half years older than my father, three inches shorter, and a bit stockier, he is often regarded as a pallid also-ran, a disappointing prototype of the Apollonian finished product who happened to be his younger brother. I suspect Moon had a rather different view.

Moon not only looked a lot like Jack, he shared his father's mordant wit and basic cynicism. He was a mischief maker, a prankster and joker. He was not untalented but careless with his gifts. Little brother Dutch might struggle to earn the distinction of a football letter, grinding it out on the line; Moon would effortlessly star at end, then get kicked off the team for smoking cigarettes. He treated schoolwork in a similar offhand manner, but still managed to bring home As, just like Dutch. My father would pursue a career in show business, but even when they were boys, it was obvious that Moon was the one who had inherited Jack's lilting Irish tenor and Nelle's grace as a dancer. He was bright. He was funny. He harbored a streak of meanness. It's not at all clear that he and my father were especially friendly.

Growing up, I could count on seeing my uncle Moon (and his wife, my aunt Bess) exactly twice a year: on Christmas day, when they visited our home, and on Thanksgiving, when we made the drive to theirs. Moon and Bess lived in one of the less posh sections of the wealthy Bel Air neighborhood of Los Angeles. Their house, a modest rambler, had a decidedly fifties decor — it appeared to have been thrown together by the set designer for *Ozzie and Harriet,* then entombed in amber. During my occasional afternoons and evenings with them, Moon and Bess were always cordial, but I never got the impression they looked forward to seeing me or would know what to do with me if we found ourselves alone together. They were not the sort of childless aunt and uncle who hungrily seek out substitute children on whom to shower their pent-up love. My parents, for their parts, seemed to regard our visits to Moon's home with a twinge of foreboding.

Moon's singing days ended before I came to know him, as a bout with cancer had required the removal of some of his vocal cords. His resulting raspiness, however, did not deter him, when presented with a captive audience, from launching into agonizingly long-winded tales, which typically ended with Moon's realizing what a damn fool somebody was. Whereas my father's stories had the benefit of pace and a punch line — a finale you could count on to be entertaining even if, as was frequently the case, you had heard it before — slogging through one of Moon's dinner table performances was like hiking toward a high mountain pass: Just when you thought relief was around the bend, there would be yet another ridge to surmount. Adding to the discomfort was a sense, subtle yet unavoidable, that the Reagan brothers had not quite put their sibling competition behind them — and never would.

During their Dixon days, as before, Moon was recognizably the bad boy of the family. In retrospect, he may have been one of those people who, proceeding through adulthood, never again attains the magic chemistry of his high school glory days. But he had a good run. Older Dixonites still marvel at his greatest practical joke, a legend that has been passed down from their parents' generation. The town awoke one morning to find that Moon and a few of his gang — though no one could pin it on them at the time — had somehow managed to get a mule-drawn wagon onto the roof of their school building.

Nobody could figure out how they did it, and it took some doing to reverse the procedure (mules being disagreeable about descending stairs). Moon had encouraged Dutch to join the prank, but his kid brother had refused, citing the certain alarm and discomfort to be felt by the mule's owner. He may also have recalled a previous occasion when he'd been a more willing accomplice in Moon's escapades.

One July, as the Fourth approached, Moon handed his little brother some fireworks — "torpedoes" my father would later call them — and goaded him into setting them off down by the Galena Avenue Bridge. Fireworks had, by this time, followed liquor onto the roster of the town's banned pleasures. Dixon's sheriff happened by in his car just as Dutch unleashed his celebration of America's independence. Flashing his badge, he instructed our young hoodlum to climb into the backseat for a ride to the police station. My father, in what may be his single recorded attempt at civil disobedience, replied, "Twinkle, twinkle little star. Who the hell do you think you are?" This unaccustomed brazenness — the flip side of the solitary boy dreaming among his bird's eggs and butterflies — didn't go over well. Ronald Reagan, even as a kid, wasn't cut out to wear a black hat — not even when show-ing off for his older brother. Jack brought him home from the station that night after paying a $14.75 fine, a hefty sum in those days. Moon and his buddies, meanwhile, had retired, snickering, to the local soda shop for ice cream.

Edmund Morris was among the last of my father's biographers to speak with con-temporaries of the Reagan boys while they were vital enough to share their memories. Perusing the footnotes of his *Dutch,* a dia-mond mine of family arcana, I come across a reference to interviews he conducted with various acquaintances of Moon's from the old days. Moon is remembered for his intel-ligence and forceful personality, but also as being somewhat cold — a young man who used humor to belittle, whose teasing was not good-natured. One of his old Eureka frat brothers, William McClellan, remembers that Moon's "needling manner . . . could bring Dutch to tears." As late as their college years, my father's older brother could make him cry.

I'm not sure Dad ever fully recovered from or forgave those taunts. Reading Morris's notes and thinking about the subtle tension I perceived between my father and uncle, it occurs to me why Moon made my parents so uncomfortable: No man is a hero to his valet . . . or his elder sibling. Moon had been present since the beginning. He knew all my father's secrets and had seen Dad not as a heroic figure but as a scared kid burying his snuffling, tear-streaked face in Nelle's apron. It had often enough been he who had made the tears come, having mercilessly bullied the hero-to-be. My father preferred that people imagine he had always been, more or less, his mature, well-fortified self. Moon knew better. His every smirking glance would have been a dart targeting the heart of Dad's carefully crafted sense of self.

A photographic portrait of the two brothers, dressed in white tie and tails on the night of my father's first presidential inauguration, is revealing. Moon's face is divided: The left side wears his trademark smirk, amped up for the occasion; the right side is a cold-blooded mask. My father, with Moon at his left shoulder, is gamely trying for a forced smile, but the corners of his mouth won't quite turn upward. He seems atypically clenched and ill at ease. My mother, with her unerring instinct for threats to her husband's equilibrium, understood the effect his brother had on him. If anything, she was more wary of him than my father.

Moon died in 1996, a victim, like his

brother, of Alzheimer's disease. The two men maintained their arm's-length relationship to the end. Dad once told me, in one of those fits of frustration I seemed to induce in him, "You're my son, so I have to love you. But sometimes you make it very hard to like you." I suspect he felt the same way about his brother.

I return to Hennepin Avenue later that night, after the house has been locked up. Starting a couple of blocks to the north between Seventh and Eighth streets, I walk the route my father would have taken on his way home from the YMCA "one cold, blustery, winter's night" in 1922, when he had just turned 11. If the reconstruction of the balustrade facing the street is accurate, he'd have needed to reach at least the corner of his property before trouble became visible in the form of a shapeless mass blocking the way inside.

So begins the iconic story from my father's youth, recounted in both autobiographies: Dutch comes home to discover his father passed out drunk on the front porch, "flat on his back . . . and no one there to lend a hand but me." This is Dutch's coming-of-age moment, the hinge on which his young life swings — the first instance, as he tells it, in which he awakens to adult responsibility.

Although Prohibition had become the law of the land the year Jack moved his family to Dixon, it would have been no harder for him to find a speakeasy in his new town than in any other in the well-liquored nation. America was embarking on a futile 13-year experiment with celebrity gangsters, bootlegging, and bathtub gin. But Dutch's immediate concern in the matter was boozily snoring away no farther than his doorstep, as he recounts in *An American Life:*

"I leaned over to see what was wrong and smelled whiskey. . . . For a moment or two, I looked down at him and thought about continuing on into the house and going to bed, as if he weren't there."

And from *Where's the Rest of Me?:*

[S]omeplace along the line to each of us, I suppose, must come that first moment of accepting responsibility. If we don't accept it (and some don't), then we must just grow older without quite growing up. I felt myself fill with grief for my father at the same time I was feeling sorry for myself. Seeing his arms spread out as if he were crucified [Dad would not be the last to mine that particular metaphorical vein] . . . I could feel no resentment against him.

Consider the embarrassment of returning home to stumble over your very own father drunkenly sprawled out at the front door, an inebriate tableau on display before the whole neighborhood. What young child wouldn't tremble with confused rage upon finding himself in such a humiliating, untenable position? Boys don't want to feel pity for their fathers; they want to feel pride. When that pride is thwarted, they'll feel anger instead, whether or not they want to admit it.

So what did Dutch do? Well, for one thing, he makes a few cuts to the story line: "I got a fistful of his overcoat. Opening the door, I managed to drag him inside and get him to bed . . . and never mentioned the incident to my mother."

Dutch did what heroes do: He manned up, took charge, muscled his pop to bed, and spared his mother's feelings besides. Only it didn't happen that way — it *couldn't* have happened that way. My father, just turned 11, was small for his age; he'd have stood maybe five feet tall and weighed barely 90 pounds. Jack, nearing 40, probably tipped the scales at 180. Dutch wasn't big or strong enough to drag Jack anywhere, not over the threshold and into the front hall, and certainly not up the narrow, angled stairway to his parents' bedroom.

So what happened?

Dutch must have woken Jack. Maybe he nudged him with his foot or clutched his lapels and given him a shake. Dutch may have been frightened to tears or he might have already retreated into himself, offering his bleary-eyed father nothing but an inscrutable mask. Jack would have lurched to his feet — probably tossing out a few choice epithets — shaken off the snow, and stumbled up to bed. But what did he say to his son? Was he angry? Contrite? Did he swear? Attempt a joke? There is no way to know, because Jack's actual role during this incident has effectively been edited out of my father's internal script.

Nobody likes Jack — not in my family, anyway. When I pursue the subject of Jack with my mother, her tone turns slightly chilly and reserved. It doesn't help that he represents the considerable portion of my father's life that unfolded before she came on the scene. More than that, she sees Jack as a drunkard and ne'er-do-well, someone who caused her husband pain. None of these are among her favorite qualities. But in fact she never knew Jack, who died of heart failure in 1941, nearly a decade before my parents met. Nelle, whom she did know, wouldn't have bad-mouthed her husband, and Moon, too, was his father's defender. The only way my mother — and, by extension, the rest of us — could have gotten a negative impression of Jack was through his other son, Ronald.

Not that Dad intentionally set about destroying his father's reputation. Quite the contrary: He never failed to acknowledge Jack's good qualities, if he seldom lingered on them. It was more his repeated expressions of pity for Jack — never anger, lest we forget — that suggested that my father considered him a sad and troubling disappointment. Perhaps most unforgivable, in Dad's reckoning, was the fact that his father was a man who made life much harder than it needed to be for the long-suffering Nelle. Jack was reduced in Dad's life reel not to bit player status but to the role of a stock character: the hardworking, hard-drinking son of Irish immigrants who pisses his dreams away in an endless round of clamoring dives and speakeasies. He has ambitious dreams but try as he might, he'll be brought down by an inability to control his baser urges. He's basically good-hearted, but undisciplined and weak. Although he never overstated any of this, there was just something in the sadness with which Dad treated the subject that made you feel sympathy not for Jack, but for him. There was 11-year-old

Dutch, shivering on his front porch, wanting nothing more than to go inside to warmth and safety, where he could slather a slice of bread with butter and then mound it with sugar — a favorite treat — before burrowing under the covers and into the fantasies of Edgar Rice Burroughs; and there was Jack, slobbering on his collar and belching up corn whiskey, blocking his son's way. This, we all understood, was not an isolated lapse. Dutch loved Christmas, but holidays were a likely time for Jack to drink. So his young son was "always torn between looking forward to Christmas and being afraid of its arrival."

The more I look into my father's history, though, the more I'm inclined to cut Jack a bit more slack than his son did.

By the standards of the day — both before and after Prohibition — Jack was hardly a world champion tippler. There is no evidence he was a true alcoholic; he could drink and stop himself before becoming completely drunk, and even my father acknowledged that Jack would sometimes go "for a couple of years without a drop." Jack usually indulged when life seemed good. He would repair to the pub, or to some hidden cellar club, to spend a bit of time with the boy-o's and come ambling home at sunup "or maybe several days later."

Jack's bonhomie surely masked deep sorrow. Not only had he lost both parents by the time he was six years old, but both his sisters, Catherine ("Catey") and Anna, appear to have died, respectively, in 1901 and 1903, at ages 22 and 18. And if he needed an object lesson in the dangers of drink, he could look to the example of his brother, William. In 1914 Jack petitioned a judge to take over his brother's finances. William had for some years been eking out a living as a cigar maker in Fulton, occupying a little store next door to his aunt Mary and aunt Margaret's millinery shop. All the while he was drinking himself crazy — literally. In 1920 Jack would have him committed to the Dixon Home for the Feeble-Minded with a diagnosis of "alcoholic psychosis." Five years later, at the age of 45, William would die there.

Jack's drinking was obviously a source of tension between him and Nelle, but it might not have been the only one. No one but a husband and wife truly knows what goes on inside their marriage. Jack was devoted to Nelle and would remain with her till death. But there may have been other issues unsettling their relationship — even driving Jack toward drink — that went unmentioned.

You'll recall that, after giving birth to my father, Nelle had been advised by her doctor not to have any more children. Given the state of contraception in those days — not to mention Nelle's extreme modesty (she used to disrobe only after shutting herself in a closet) — it's possible that by the time they reached their late twenties, Jack and Nelle's sex life had effectively come to an end.

Not one bit of this was broached during my father's discussions of Jack as I was growing up. None of us — my mother included — even knew that Jack had a brother and sisters (my great-uncle and great-aunts). We certainly weren't apprised of their tragic early ends. Was my father aware of them? Would Jack and Nelle have kept William's fate a secret from their boys? Were his sisters' deaths too painful for Jack to recount? Or were William, Catey, and Anna — and the more complicated aspects of his parents' marriage — among the many unhelpful distractions that were, like the details of that cold night on the front porch, simply omitted from Dad's story?

Jack was not without his flaws. He drank during an age when men imbibed far more alcohol, on average, than in today's more abstemious climate. Sometimes he drank to excess. But in no sense does he appear to

166

have been an uncaring father or an unloving husband. He came from nothing, and nearly his entire family had died around him by the time he reached adulthood. For all his rough edges, his bawdiness and gimlet-eyed view of life, he possessed an innate dignity. He had a sense of style, a mind open to possibility. If he was weak, he was also principled. If he transgressed, he was, as well, a faithful and diligent provider. I can't fault Dutch for being disappointed by his father's lapses; I only wish Dad had been able to reconcile his feelings for Jack so we all might have enjoyed him more thoroughly for the man he was.

Dutch might not have told his mother about the front porch incident with Jack, but that hardly would have been necessary. Nelle could read the signs. Jack wasn't putting anything over on her; neither was Dutch. Coming home that evening to find a besotted husband and somber child, she would have had no trouble drawing the likely conclusion.

Her response, a short time later, was to place into her younger son's hands an inspirational tome, *That Printer of Udell's*. First published in 1902, it is the work of Harold Bell Wright, a well-known and prolific spiritual author of the day. To modern sensibilities, the book is virtually impenetrable. But several of its features — as Nelle surely appreciated — resonated with Dutch.

The novel's hero, Dick Falkner, leaves home after watching his beloved mother expire — even as his father, who has "Bin down ter th' stillhouse all evenin'," snores menacingly in a corner. Mother and son have both suffered terribly "from his drunken father's rage." After a few years of wandering, during which Dick samples the "evil, degrading things" on offer in large cities — and which lurk inescapably in men's hearts — he is presented the opportunity for an epiphany. One cold night, passing a church on his way home, Dick's mentor, printing shop owner George Udell, discovers "a dark form half hidden in the snow piled about the doorway of the building." (Imagine Dutch's shudder of recognition upon reading that line!) A homeless man has frozen to death no more than a few steps from a House of God. Dick joins Udell at the undertaker's. Wright tells us that Dick "seemed strangely moved as he bent over the casket." In the man's tragic end, Dick perceives the hypocrisy inherent in much organized religion: "This awful neglect and indifference comes from a *lack* of Christ's teaching, or rather from a lack of the application of Christ's teaching and too much teaching of the church. The trouble is that people follow the church and not Christ; they become church members, but not Christians."

Dick, believing that "it is contrary to God's law that the *helpless* should go hungry," nonetheless perceives indigents as belonging to "two classes . . . the deserving and undeserving." The undeserving, he feels, benefit from policies that "encourage the idle in their idleness," while the deserving suffer neglect. He proposes the town furnish the worthy poor — but not the idlers — with a sort of group home, where they will make themselves useful collecting scrap wood and rendering it into marketable kindling. This endeavor, Dick is certain, will prepare them for a productive role in society. Just who will separate the worthy sheep from the idle goats — and by what criteria — is left unexplained.

Udell's heroic printer has been seen by some as an early template for my father's later conservatism. The notion of a class of needy people we can safely ignore without undermining our consciences mirrors a certain strain of conservative thought that sees those at the bottom of the economic ladder as having ended up there by dint of their own moral laxity. But that conservatism was decades in the future, long after this book had become a footnote in his memory. Connecting Dick Falkner's undeserving poor and my father's later employment of the "welfare queen" trope is surely stretching things.

Likewise, Dick's eventually leaving the printer's shop for "a field of wider usefulness at the National Capitol" has also been noted, though I hardly think my father took this as a cue for his own later move into politics. If Wright's novel shaped anything, it was more likely Dad's approach to religion.

Potentially discomfiting, I imagine, to many current social conservatives is Wright's portrayal of organized religion as a bastion of hypocrisy and church members as "the biggest frauds in the world." His book is, rather, a manifesto for "practical Christianity." Pious talk is all well and good, and declaring Jesus to be your savior is fine but, in the end, deeds are what count — get out there and help the needy! Nelle, like much of Wright's readership, might have understood this as a broadside primarily aimed at the Catholic Church.

Nelle's purpose in giving her son this book was almost certainly more to soothe than to foster a religious conversion. In keeping with the doctrine of the Disciples, she believed her son should make up his own mind about matters of spirituality, and it didn't take long for him to do so. Inspired by Wright's novel and still shaken by the incident with Jack, Dutch soon approached his mother and said, "I want to declare my faith and be baptized." He even convinced Moon to join him. On June 21, 1922 — the solstice — Dutch and Moon donned their bathing suits and headed up South Hennepin Avenue to Dixon's First Christian Church for a full immersion. The news was kept from Jack, who would have been tempted to remind his older son that he'd already been baptized a Catholic — a complicating factor that seems to have been withheld from Moon by his mother. When Moon later learned the truth, it would leave him with bitter, resentful feelings toward Nelle.

That Printer of Udell's might have provided an early mold for my father's spiritual sensibilities — a sincere but low-key nonexhibitionist approach he maintained throughout his life. No religious harangues echoed through our house as I grew up. Dad didn't shout hosannas. He was a man of faith, but it was a quiet faith built around a basic do unto others philosophy. By the age of four I had gathered that his religion involved someone Dad fondly referred to as the "Man upstairs," a seemingly benevolent figure I conflated, in a vague way, with Santa Claus. Religion itself was, for me, a fidgety, buttock-numbing weekend obligation. Every Sunday morning the family would dress up, pile into the car — eventually an official state limo — and head off to the 11 o'clock service. Until I had to go and become a heretic.

"Come on, get your clothes on. We're leaving for church."

"I'm not going."

Dad's face hardly registered this declaration — I might just as well have announced an intention to self-immolate. "Hurry up! Put your suit on!"

I had been pondering, in my 12-year-old way, my growing discomfort with Dad's faith for some time. I had concluded that the deity most folks professed to worship was a fiction. This god might impel them toward good — or bad — acts, but it was a figment of their imagination nonetheless. You didn't have to be a biblical scholar to realize that the combination of Old and New Testaments was a hodgepodge of contradictions.

"No. I don't believe in all that anymore. I'm not going to sit there and pretend. I'm not going."

As my words finally began to penetrate, I

saw washing across Dad's face emotions that began with profound dismay but then transformed into a more hopeful determination. Having quickly discarded the idea of dragging his 12-year-old son flailing and hollering into church for an emergency exorcism, he wisely let the matter go for the moment. But as he turned toward me on the way out of my bedroom door for one last worried look, I knew we'd only completed round one.

Church for us was the Bel Air Presbyterian. I'm not sure why my parents had chosen this particular one, a half hour from our home in Pacific Palisades — were there no closer churches? But before a certain age, you don't question such things. Worship took place in a drearily modern structure heaved up in one of those spasms of dubious architectural taste common to the late fifties and early sixties. Over the years the building had developed a number of alarming fissures in its plaster as well as some intriguingly shaped water stains, which at least served to occupy the desperate juvenile imagination. The entire structure was painted in depressing, grayish neutral tones. Its ceiling vaulted without exalting. The overall effect, when combined with some singularly unevocative stained-glass designs, was less a state of grace than a profoundly enervating ennui.

There were blessed moments of levity, however unintentional. For a time, one of the middle-aged women in the choir provided a welcome dash of lunacy. She had, it became apparent, developed an unbridled crush on my father. Every hymn of praise was suddenly, in her rendition, beamed directly toward Dad. Her wet, limpid eyes would remain fixed on him for the entire lengthy service. Dad, with his performer's graciousness toward other performers, could not bring himself to look away from the choir when they sang. But he strained to acknowledge them without meeting the eye of — and thereby encouraging — his lovesick admirer. No matter; she took to ambushing him at the door on his way out. We countered, on subsequent Sundays, by dashing for the rear entrance, then mixing up our escape routes. Finally, one weekend at the ranch, as we were checking the water level of a pond in one of the lower pastures, we looked up to see her peering at us from the shoulder of the road above with the aid of high-powered binoculars. Sadly, that episode resulted in the poor woman's leaving the choir for an enforced "sabbatical."

Looking back, it's hard to believe I was willing to give all that up over a little thing like absence of faith.

Upon returning from church the day of my refusal to attend, Dad took another pass at his apostate son — to no avail. He next adopted a strategy of lying low, acknowledging my transgression with little more than the occasional wistful glance, allowing time for the awful reality of my decision to weigh on me. Then, when he reckoned I'd twisted in the icy, shrieking void of godlessness long enough, he brought in a ringer.

I was informed one otherwise normal afternoon that Donn Moomaw, former all-star lineman for the University of California, Los Angeles, Bruins, and my erstwhile pastor, would be dropping by our house to have a chat with me. Donn was a towering, square-jawed fellow with hands that looked as if they could pulp coconuts. He had a booming voice and an avuncular, jockish manner. Dad had tremendous regard for his rhetorical skills; it wouldn't surprise me if he had made a few mental crib notes during sermons. Donn was extremely popular with his congregation. (A bit too popular, as it turned out, for he would eventually step down when it came to light that he'd been shepherding certain members of his flock in carnal fashion.) He was just the man to instill a sense of virile Christianity in a young man drifting haplessly toward the slathering maw of hell.

Whatever Dad had expected from it, I found the encounter strangely exhilarating. After a moment or two of wondering whether Donn would unroll some argument I couldn't counter — he was a professional, after all — I relaxed and began to enjoy our bantering, mildly argumentative exchange. I was holding my own and, what's more, could tell that Donn's heart wasn't really in the fight. I teased him about the notion of God as a male figure: If He wasn't also female (and any other gender that might arise in the universe), wasn't He, therefore, less than infinite? Donn bore my adolescent jibes with good humor. Before long we lapsed into talking football. When the good reverend finally made his escape, Dad was crestfallen to find his faithless son unbowed.

More than a decade later, at my sister Patti's wedding, Donn would confess his embarrassment to me. "I gotta tell you, that afternoon made me really uncomfortable. But your dad was just so worried about you." No harm done, I told him. I'm still an atheist. We laughed about the incident.

Dad, meanwhile, never gave up hope that I'd come back to the Man upstairs.

■ ■ ■ ■

Dutch never questioned the existence of a benevolent deity. He faithfully attended his mother's church, eventually joining her in readings before the congregation. On Easter Sunday 1926, age 15, he led the church's sunrise service in prayer as its members gathered midspan on the Hennepin Avenue Bridge. But religion does not seem to have dominated my father's daily life, as other activities loomed large. There were sports to be played. As always, nearby woods needed exploring. There was a river whose waters he would swim in summer, whose frozen stretches he would skate across come winter, his jacket, held wide open, billowing with a frigid wind that propelled him downstream. With his brother and friends he occasionally caddied at the local country club north of town. He spent one summer doing pick and shovel work for a residential contractor before finding more rewarding employment as a lifeguard at the city's Lowell Park. As alluring as the river, the Dixon Public Library beckoned with countless volumes of adventure and derring-do. The Dixon Theater downtown offered a newer and utterly mesmerizing avenue for his imagination — and his first view of the West — in the cowboy capers of Tom Mix and other serials. And when he'd had enough of reading, running around, and soaking in flickering images projected on a screen, he could always club a few rabbits.

This was an activity — not uncommon in the days of Dad's youth — that would certainly strike all but the most rural of today's youngsters as decidedly off-putting. In the earliest preserved sample of my father's writing, an 11-year-old Dutch pencils a letter to a couple of high school girls, Gladys Shippert and her sister Alma ("To my Lady Fair and her Sister"), who had attended the First Christian Church with him in Dixon before moving away. Amid a number of bulletins concerning the local school's football fortunes he mentions his efforts to stock the family larder: "I have 12 rabbits and I am going to kill and eat them." Moon had built a rabbit hutch behind a small barn/garage at the back of the Hennepin property as well as a coop for pigeons within. The meat on the Reagans' dinner table was often as fresh as could be. In case the two young women missed his point, Dutch appendead a postscript: "Smell that meat/ Aint It good."

By the fall of 1924 the Reagans had moved across the river so the boys could attend the better regarded Dixon High School North

Side. Moon, however, opted to remain with his pals on the south side, meaning the brothers would be split academically for the first time. The backyard of their new rental on Everett Street overlooked the playfield at Dutch's new high school. Comfortable as ever whiling away time in solitary pursuits, my father would spend hours on the embankment above the field with a fishing rod, casting sticks for the family dog, a Boston terrier named Mr. Jiggs, to retrieve, then reeling him in.

It was in Dixon that my father discovered a world where objects could be seen at a distance, where the fields spreading beyond his cozy grid of streets ended in a definite horizon. Driving out of town one day, wondering why Moon could read street signs that were nothing but an indistinct blur to him, Dutch idly slipped on a pair of Nelle's spectacles: "I suddenly saw a glorious, sharply outlined world jump into focus and shouted with delight." He would be less enamored of the heavy eyeglasses he needed to wear.

It was in Dixon, too, that Dutch became smitten by his first serious girlfriend — the daughter, as it happens, of his First Christian Church pastor, the formidable Ben H. Cleaver. Margaret ("Mugs") Cleaver was a bright, energetic girl with dark, wavy hair, brown eyes, and a forceful personality. She was also, by all accounts I've read, a rather humorless young lady. This might have made her an odd match for Dutch, who valued people who laughed at his jokes. But Mugs must have found plenty to like in the tall, handsome boy with thick hair, a ready grin, and a fluid, economical way of moving that suggested he just might go places. He, too, was bright, but not diligent enough to challenge her academic superiority. He was interested in things beyond their little city. He was polite, too — not like his needling bully of a brother. You didn't have to worry about him getting fresh, either.

One afternoon in the summer of 1927, a local woman named Elizabeth ("Bee") Frey took her Kodak Brownie camera down to the beach at Lowell Park. Three of the photos she snapped that day are displayed in the Hennepin house. One is the well-known shot of my father at 16, squinting into the sun with the river at his back, looking ridiculously tanned and handsome in his lifeguard singlet. A second, seldom reproduced, catches him in action, leaping into a canoe with a fellow lifeguard. The third is most intriguing: Dutch and a young woman are standing beneath an oak tree; her arms are locked around his torso in a bear hug while his left hand, reaching around behind, strays dangerously south along her flank. Generally either sober or gamely smiling for photographers, here my father is doing some full-on teenage mugging — with mouth agape and eyes bugging. The young woman's face, seemingly older and more assured beneath her tight-fitting bathing cap, barely registers a smile. Who is she? A caption elsewhere identifies her as Dutch's cousin. But that hand of my father's doesn't appear to be heading into cousin territory. Something in her level gaze, in the unapologetic possessiveness with which she tugs my father toward her, tells me she might be Mugs. On the other hand, Mugs preferred more high-minded pursuits to a frolic at the beach.

While they were, in many respects, an odd pair, Dutch and Mugs nevertheless became inseparable through high school and college. They were active in their high school's Dramatic Society, appearing together in school plays. Both worked on the *Dixonian,* the school yearbook. She did most of the writing; as art director, he gave the book a cinematic theme, hinting at a fascination he was still keeping largely under wraps. Mugs was elected president of her senior class; Dutch became student body president. She is identified in the 1928 yearbook as "Our

Popular All-Around Everything." The quote he chose to accompany his senior picture is more whimsical: "Life is just one grand sweet song, so let's start the music."

Dixon gossips assured one another the two would eventually wed. Whatever the outcome, it was generally recognized that Mugs was calling the shots. After hearing gossip about one of Jack's benders, Mugs threatened to end the relationship. She wasn't buying my father's explanation about alcoholism as a sickness and Jack being an object of pity not resentment. Crushed, Dutch informed Nelle that if his father's drinking cost him his girl, he and Jack would never speak again. Mugs eventually got over her anger at Jack, but it was neither the first nor last time my father found himself under the sway of a petite, dark-eyed, highly motivated woman.

My last night in Dixon, I end up back at the Hennepin house. It has been closed for hours, so I head into the park occupying the lot next door and settle onto a bench beneath my father's statue. Why is it that artists, particularly sculptors, have such a hard time capturing Dad's likeness? The bronze face hovering over me belongs to the comedic actor Larry Storch, or perhaps Larry

Hagman. Even Dad's White House portrait had to be sent back for a redo after the first version turned out to be a dead ringer for Arthur Godfrey.

Inhaling the freshness of the night air, I look northward past Dutch's old home down Hennepin Avenue. Again, I imagine my 11-year-old father hurrying along the snow-covered sidewalk, bundled against the cold in coat and scarf, woolen newsboy cap pulled down over tingling ears, mind whirring with thoughts of adventures he, Ronald Wilson Reagan, is just the lad to undertake. So far in his young life he has been largely insulated from life's vagaries. His narrative, still in its storyboard stage, has not required drastic editing. As the hero of his tale, he has not faced anything more daunting than grass snakes and school bullies. I can picture him now in the last instant before all that changes.

As little Dutch reaches his porch, but before his blurry vision resolves the figure crumpled at the doorstep, I shake myself. I don't want to witness his jagged shock, that moment when some precious space in him seals itself shut forever. Spinning ahead just a few years, I replace the younger Dutch with a more mature version (in reality, he'd have been walking home along Everett by this time, but I'm allowing myself some liberties). I melt the snow, inviting spring to return. Dutch's winter attire is replaced with a light jacket, collar raffishly upturned. His hair, colored like Nelle's but with a mind of its own like Jack's, ruffles over his forehead. With his new, thick-framed glasses, he should have no trouble spotting me on my bench (though he'll be surprised to find that his neighbor's house has unaccountably vanished). He is taller now, though still a couple of inches shy of six feet. His limbs are still those of a stripling, but his shoulders have begun to broaden, and he has already acquired the unhurried, ground-covering stride of his adult years. Only recently has he discovered that he is handsome. He carries himself with a newly minted air of confidence — some observers might even detect a trace of cockiness. Dixon has been good to him, and he has begun to think that he might just be good for Dixon — or even places beyond. He is beginning to stand out as a young man of promise, just as Nelle had always insisted he would.

Perhaps in response to his family's migrations and chaotic emotional tides, Dutch has come to value order and regularity in his life. His grades are good, but he's drawn more to extracurricular pursuits. While not a meticulous organizer, he is becoming aware of his ability to get people engaged by using the force of his personality. He is obsessed with the game of football, seeing it as a test of manhood and an avenue to public acclaim. He has also developed a strong, almost patriotic affinity for the institutions to which he belongs, particularly his school.

Those threads intertwine in an essay entitled "School Spirit," written during his junior year at Dixon High North Side. In this two-page paper he laments the passing of the "old tradition" and fears that loyalty to the Purple and White (Dixon High's colors) has been "buried beneath a cloak of attempted sophistication that sneers at this show of feelings." In the midst of the Jazz Age — his generation's version of the 1960s — Dutch is identifying with the sort of kids who will one day react to rock music by clutching tight their Pat Boone records. "Do not think I am sentimental or holding myself as an example," he writes, tipping the reader to the certainty of both. "But the fellow who knows the smell of liniment, and the salty tang of sweat-soaked jerseys, has acquired something precious, which no one can steal." By being "battered and bruised for two years," Dutch assures us, this fellow will know a "love and loyalty . . . as true as the temper of a fine steel blade." He will find that "love of school has become a religion with him."

The paper is well written; it receives a 94. But even Dutch's teacher finds his earnest tone worth questioning. "I wonder what changes will come in your standards of values," she writes along the margin, "8 years from now?"

Not many, I want to tell her.

To be sure Dutch's head still wanders a stratosphere where he is the stuff of Arthurian legend. His fertile imagination is stoked by novels and movies, his mind still filled with boyish fantasies. But he has learned that some dreams are practical and, what's more, have a price he can meet. His town has recently given him an opportunity to prove his mettle, placing the lives of citizens and visitors alike in his young hands. All along, he has been eager to prove himself capable of acting as a true hero. Now, he will have his chance.

Jack Reagan (second from right) with his siblings and two young cousins in the late 1890s. His older brother, William (left), drank himself to death. His sisters appear to have died young only a few years after this photo was taken.

Jack as a teenager. He never attended high school or college.

Jack's father, John Michael Reagan, came to America in 1859. He died of TB when Jack was six.

Nelle and Jack as newlyweds.

Nelle's piety, if not her compositional skills, are evident in her poetry.

A Sonnet — By Nellie Reagan

When I consider how my life is spent
The most that I can do will be to prove
Tis by His side, each day, I seek to move.
To higher, nobler things my mind is bent
Thus giving of my strength, which God has lent,
I strive some needy souls unrest, to soothe
Lest they the path of righteousness shall lose
Through fault of mine, my Maker to present.
If I should fail to show them of their need
How could I hope to meet Him face to face.
As give a just account of all my ways.
In thought of mind, in work, and in each deed
My life must prove the power of His grace
By every action through my living days.

My father's first hometown: Tampico, Illinois, in the early twentieth century.

Tampico around the time of my father's birth. Nelle has marked with an X the Reagan family apartment.

"Suppose you know that fellow in his shirtsleeves . . ." Jack in front of the H. C. Pitney store, Tampico.

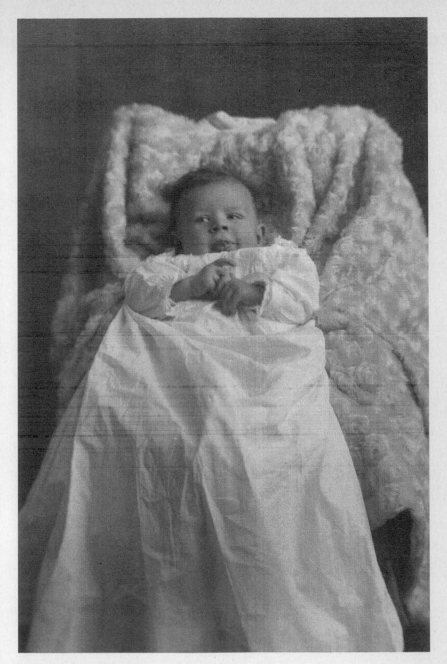

Dutch Reagan, newly arrived.

Can you pick out the future president? (Middle row, eighth from left.)

Dutch airborne above the Rock River c. 1930. The dock and water slide are long gone.

My father took to horseback riding with enthusiasm at a fairly early age. Here he's in equestrian outfit in Dixon in the early 1930s.

Dutch onstage (center, in tuxedo) performing in a school play at North Dixon High School.

Dutch and Moon on the Dixon High football squad. Dutch is a freshman, Moon a junior.

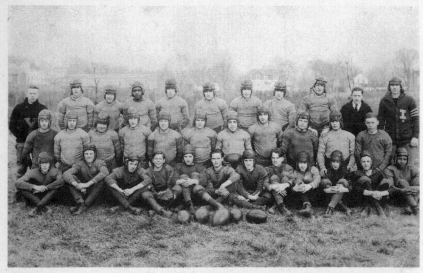

③ A.Bowers   J. Kennedy   H.Coss 'Wmk' McKeynolds   G.O'Malley   C.Keyes   R. McNichols
      M.Kinney 'Moon' Regan   C.Fisher   Bo' Culley   ②M.Keller   F.Kellar   L.Miller
   G. McNichols   B.Johnson   'Buns' Kerst   G.Bande   H.Wennman   Wilson   H.Marks E.Beach
   ① ?   D.Miller   Gerdes   R.Reagan   ?   Dawson   ?   ?   K.Segner J.Padgett ? F.Spatts

My father, newly graduated from Eureka College and ready for a career in radio (and beyond).

Ronald Reagan as a young Hollywood hunk.

Dad with his father, Jack, in Los Angeles. The first and only home Jack ever owned was the one his son bought for him with money from his first Warner Bros. contract.

My father with his parents shortly after signing a contract with Warner Bros.

Nelle Reagan.

My father and mother honeymooning in Waikiki, Hawaii, 1952.

Breakfast at the Reagans' courtesy of General Electric, c. 1960. When Dad hosted GE Theater on television, the company built him a home stocked with all the latest electric gadgets. I apparently approved.

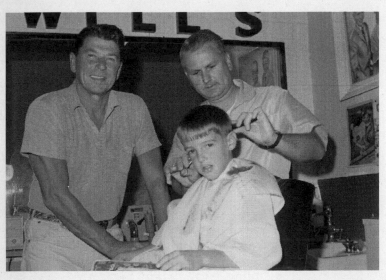

Two of us seem to be enjoying ourselves: a classic Dad and lad moment.

Gubernatorial campaign publicity shot, 1966. You can tell how thrilled I am to have gotten gussied up for the photographer.

Hitting the governor of California (my father) with my first ever snowball.

My father moments after rescuing this little girl from the bottom of our Sacramento swimming pool during a backyard party.

Dad and me in the Oval Office — my bow-tie is a clip-on satire of a then-current conservative affectation.

CHAPTER SIX
LOCAL HERO

In the spring of 1926 Jack Reagan took his son Dutch to meet with Ed Graybill and his wife, Ruth. The Graybills managed the beach and ran the concession stand at Lowell Park, the swimming and recreation spot north of Dixon, on the Rock River's Grand Detour. Dutch, already recognized as an unusually gifted swimmer, had recently completed lifeguard training at the Dixon YMCA, a rigorous program that required him to demonstrate proficiency in a number of rescue techniques as well as artificial respiration. The lifeguard job at the park offered $18 a week — a good paycheck at a time when many people worked for a dollar a day, and it was money the Reagan family could use. Included in the deal would be all the nickel root beers and ten-cent hamburgers piled high with relish, pickles, and onions a hungry lifeguard could manage to scarf down. The hours were long: 10:00 A.M. till the last swimmers left the water — as late as 10:00 P.M. on sultry evenings — seven days a week. Dutch wanted the job.

He might have been a talented swimmer, and he might have earned his lifeguard certificate from the Y, but Dutch Reagan was barely 15 years old. He'd just finished his sophomore year at Dixon High. Was this really someone who could be entrusted with the safety of locals and visitors at a popular, crowded beach? Graybill was initially unconvinced. "You're pretty young," he told the thin, earnest teenager standing before him. But Jack spoke up for his son: "He can do it; give the boy a chance."

On my first evening in Dixon, I grab dinner at a good Mexican restaurant run by a mother-daughter team. Then, noting that there is still light in the sky, I drive out of town for a quick peek at Lowell Park. While Dad might have reckoned that he came of age one frozen evening while leaning over his drunken father, I'm more inclined to see that maturity evolving during the sweltering summers he spent keeping watch over this narrow stretch of the Rock River. I can't wait till morning to visit the spot.

In fact, I almost end up spending the night there. As I pull up to the entrance of the park, a sign warns that its automatic gate will shut at 8:00 P.M. The clock in my rental car reads 8:20; the gate stands open. Reasoning (stupidly) that either the gate must be broken or my clock is an hour fast, leaving me 40 minutes to satisfy my curiosity, I drive on. Headlights piercing the deepening twilight, I wend my way through thick woods to the shore. The park is deserted. The river, swollen with recent rains, carries downed limbs and mats of greenery on its leaden shoulders. Swallows swoop and dip over swirling eddies. More thunderstorms are predicted overnight. Reassuring myself that I'll have plenty of time to explore in the days ahead, I take another winding road back to the entrance. When I get there, my dashboard clock reads 8:50. The gate is locked tight. It is the only exit. I appear to be trapped in Lowell Park.

Prickling sweat running down my spine, I begin nervously reconnoitering the tree line that separates me from the road outside. It doesn't look good. Conifers stand thick in serried rows. Is there a ditch beyond the trees? I can't quite tell. I begin to laugh at myself, as it looks more and more like I'll face a choice between a long walk back to town or an uncomfortable night in the backseat. Being arrested for trespassing might at least get me a cot, and I begin to imagine the

inevitable humiliating headlines: DISORI-
ENTED VAGRANT IN PARK IS RONALD
REAGAN'S SON; DUTCH'S BOY DOESN'T
KNOW TIME OF DAY. That should do wonders for my marginal anonymity and endear
me to the locals besides. Finally, spotting a
narrow, curving break through the pines,
I manage a desperate off-road gambit and
scramble my way back to the pavement without doing irreparable damage to my car.

It didn't take long for the Graybills to conclude that Dutch was just the young man for
the job. "He liked it, and we liked him," remembered Ruth Graybill years later. "There
was never a basket left at closing time," she
said, referring to the containers in which
swimmers would store their clothes. "That
meant we had a good lifeguard; there were
no bodies at the bottom." Pulling floundering swimmers from the river seemed to
agree with my father; he would remember it
as "the best job I ever had." Not only that;
it would eventually earn him his first public
recognition.

Thursday morning, August 2, 1928,
dawned sticky and hot. Dutch rolled out
of bed, wolfed down some breakfast, and
grabbed his black singlet, the one-piece
bathing suit with LIFEGUARD stenciled
across the chest. Down Everett he went,

190

then south across the river heading for the Graybills' house, kitty-corner from his old grade school on Fifth Street. Just as he did every other summer morning, he helped load his bosses' truck before catching a ride with them out to the park.

Dutch liked to get to the beach a bit early. His habit was to swim the river's width across and back every morning before the crowds arrived — partly to stay fit, partly to get a feel for the water. Experience had taught him that the river had its moods. Depending on what was happening upstream — rain to the north swelling the river? — or downstream — Dixon's dam open, allowing a faster flow? — the current would be more or less treacherous, the river more or less inclined to suck swimmers into its depths. These morning swims also kept him in shape for the annual cross-river race. As far as I know, his time of 2 minutes, 11 seconds in that contest has never been bested (and probably won't be, as the river has been closed to swimming for decades due to concerns about the cleanliness of the water).

The day turned out to be a baking scorcher, just as Dutch had figured. Seeking relief from the oppressive humidity, folks from town and the surrounding countryside headed for the beach in caravans of automobiles and farm trucks. Heat like this meant swimmers would linger in the water well past sunset, meaning an extra-long evening for the lifeguard. Sometimes, when Dutch grew tired of minding the last stragglers, he'd employ a clever method of clearing them out. Stealthily he'd begin tossing pebbles into the shallows. "What was that?" the bathers would wonder. "Oh, just some ol' river rats — they come out this time of night," Lowell Park's trusty lifeguard would reply. That usually emptied the beach.

By 9:30 P.M. the "river rats" had done their job, and Dutch was ready to call it a day. Helping Ed Graybill close up the bathhouse and concession stand, he didn't see two young men and their dates sneak down and slip into the water. By that time the light had all but left the western horizon; the river flowed dark beyond the deep shadows of the oaks hugging the shore. Within minutes Dutch was alerted by a sound of splashing and flailing. Three young people emerged from the gloom, running toward him, screaming. Their friend, who was evidently not as strong a swimmer as he believed, had been pulled under.

Picture yourself at 17. Give it a second — really take yourself back to the insecure, somewhat awkward, not-nearly-as-adult-as-you-thought self that was the actual 17-year-old you. Now, imagine yourself sprinting through the night toward the bank of a rushing river. To make things more interesting, let's toss nearsightedness into the picture. You've slung aside your glasses — along with your shoes and clothes — as you race to the river's edge. The water is now nothing but a dim band amid a larger darkness. As you reach the bobbing end of a floating dock jutting into the murk, you know that somewhere in that moving mass of black water, whirling rapidly away downstream, is a drowning man. You can't see him in the blackness; in order to locate him, you must try to get a fix on the sound of his struggling. Perhaps bigger and stronger than you, he is terrified and fighting for his life. He will lunge and grasp at anything within reach with a desperate energy. In a frenzied panic to save himself, he is fully capable of drowning a would-be rescuer. Tonight, that rescuer will be you. Saving him is your summer job. Go.

JAMES RAIDER PULLED FROM THE JAWS OF DEATH read the front-page headline of the next day's edition of the *Dixon Evening Telegraph*. There had been "quite a struggle," it was reported, before "lifeguard Ronald 'Dutch' Reagan" managed to subdue

Raider and bring him to shore, pulling one-armed against the current, dragging him up the bank onto the lawn, and performing artificial respiration. After a minute or two Raider came around and was judged sound enough to be sent home. For his twenty-fifth rescue, Dutch got his first taste of public acclaim. He'd have been pleased, I think, by the attention. Except for the unusually late hour, the rescue itself may have seemed fairly routine.

From across the backyard of our house in Sacramento, I can see Dad waving jauntily to the guests at my parents' annual Fourth of July party as he heads inside to change out of the wet clothes plastered to his frame. Has he unaccountably decided to take a swim fully dressed?

With a hurried whisper, my mother fills me in as she follows behind. "Daddy just saved a little girl from drowning!"

Typical.

Not that I remembered, at age nine, ever having seen my father actually rescue anyone before. But I knew about his 77 saves at Lowell Park. Seventy-seven people pulled from the Rock River over the course of seven summers — an average of 11 per season, or around one per week. So there was nothing especially surprising about Dad's jumping into the calm, shallow water of our swimming pool to prevent a child from drowning.

"What do you love about your father?" An impertinent question from my wife, Doria, who delights in watching me squirm. That's an awfully big one. But I have no trouble acknowledging one thing I deeply appreciate: He paid attention to what was going on in the physical world around him. Two hundred people were standing idly by that afternoon in Sacramento, including the parents of the little girl in question. Who noticed, in a pool full of thrashing, splashing kids, the one child in the melee who was lingering underwater a little too long?

Seven–year-old Alicia Berry had been hanging onto the side of our pool in about four feet of water — just a bit over her head. Alicia couldn't swim. When a rubber raft drifted by she realized that if she could just get ahold of it, she could join the other kids in the middle of the pool. But as she pushed off to grab it, another child pulled the raft away. Alicia had no chance to cry out before she sank to the bottom. My father was standing nearby, chatting with some guests. In retrospect, I'm sure he had positioned himself at exactly that spot so he could keep watch over the pool. The Fourth of July bash was traditionally a big event in Sacramento political circles, involving plenty of schmoozing and shoptalk. But in Dad's mind, attending to the people — particularly children — in the water would have been the top priority. Lucky for Alicia.

While my father hadn't seen the actual mishap with the raft, he had been periodically scanning the pool, taking note of the weaker swimmers. He would have noticed Alicia. When she went under, a clock began running in his head. He probably gave her about 10 seconds to surface before politely excusing himself from his conversation and diving in. The "rescue" involved little more than scooping the little girl from the bottom and setting her on the pool's edge. "At no time was my life in danger," Dad assured the press afterward. True enough. Virtually anyone could have done it. But you had to be paying attention.

Photos taken moments later show Dad standing in water barely to his waist. Before him, a slightly dazed Alicia sits on the side of the pool with her legs dangling over the edge. Two mothers, mine and hers, hover with towels and concerned looks. By the expression on Dad's face, I can tell he's already satisfied that Alicia will be fine. Alicia's mother, it is later reported, was reluctant to let her daughter back in the water. "But," she remarked, "the governor advised me that if she was kept out she would be afraid of the water. He said, 'It's just like riding a horse. If you fall off and stay off, you'll be afraid later.'" How often had I heard *that* one, growing up?

In the background of one picture I've seen, Alicia's father appears. The look on his face is harder to read but clearly involves emotions other than relief and gratitude. If I remember correctly, he was not a big fan of Dad's. It's not hard to imagine what he might be thinking: *My political enemy plays the big hero saving my daughter's life while I'm off freshening my piña colada.* But as Dad ruefully admitted on occasion, the business of saving lives was never uncomplicated.

"Not one of them has ever thanked me," Dutch complained to his parents one day after yet another near-drowning victim had accosted him for having had the temerity to do his job. Men, in particular, were reluctant to admit that they had been in any danger — especially when their savior was young enough to be their kid brother. It was Jack who then suggested that his son begin carving notches on a handy log — one for each victim saved. "These fellas I'd pulled

197

out of the river," my father used to tell me, "would kinda sidle up to me a little later saying, 'Y'know,'" and here Dad's voice would acquire the tone of a pathetic wiseass, "'I was fine out there — didn't really need your help.' I'd just nod and keep carving my notch."

Only once was Dutch rewarded for performing a rescue. When Gus Whiffleberg went down the slide erected at the end of the Lowell Park dock, the impact as he hit the water knocked his dentures out. He paid Dutch $10 for fishing them off the bottom.

Some, looking back, have supposed that many of Dutch's 77 saves must have been bogus, involving little more than hand-holding tired bathers back to the beach from the wooden swimming platform anchored in the river. They suspect he simply liked carving those notches in his driftwood log.

But 26 years ago, on the occasion of my father's visit to Dixon to celebrate his birthday and visit his newly renovated boyhood home, Light Thompson, a friend from Lowell Park days, recalled that Dutch knew the difference between housekeeping chores and real emergencies. "If somebody was trying to make it to the raft and was having a hard time, he'd say, 'Light, give that little gal a push,' and I'd go in. But if they were going

under, he was gone, and I mean, he moved."
Thompson remembered Dutch throwing
aside his glasses with a sweeping motion
and said he retrieved the spectacles out of
the shallows for his friend on more than one
occasion.

My father may have felt, deep within, that
he was capable of heroism — may even have
been eager to act out a heroic role in life —
but résumé padding would have cut against
the grain. Being seen as a hero was all well
and good, but Dutch wanted to *feel* like a
hero. He wanted to truly be the sort of man
people have good reason to admire. That
meant adhering to a strict ethical code. Real
heroes didn't waste time showing off; they
rose to challenges confronting them. The
notches on the log had to mean something.
They couldn't be faked without fatally undermining the self he was religiously forging.
Beyond that, my father had come to value
order in all things. Someone drowning at
his beach, on his watch, would have brought
chaos to his moral universe, casting a dark
cloud over his beloved Dixon and calling
into question his own capabilities. By hurl-
ing himself into the river to save the lives of
drowning strangers, he was not only proving
his worth, he was setting the world aright.

How many of his rescues were legitimate

(allowing for a handful of young women desperate enough to be saved by such a handsome lifeguard that they got themselves in a bit more trouble than they'd bargained for)? I'd put the number at . . . 77.

Not being a believer in astrology, I don't put much credence in Dad's status as an Aquarian. Nevertheless, water was indisputably his element, and he gave it his full respect. He taught his children to do the same, seeing to it that we all knew how to swim at an early age. When we were little, in order to test our comfort in the water, he would occasionally saunter by as we lingered by the edge of the pool and give us a little hip-check into the drink. He just wanted to make sure we didn't lose our composure if we found ourselves unexpectedly submerged.

Natural bodies of water, he warned, presented extra dangers. A river might look placid on its surface, but beneath the waterline powerful currents could be running, vortices and undertows that would sap the strength of even the strongest swimmer. The shortest route from bank to bank, through moving water, my father had learned, was never a straight line. You had to work with the flow and calculate your trajectory. Never fight water, he told us; water will always be stronger than you. Ocean breakers, as they build approaching shore, will pull you toward them; don't waste energy resisting; swim out to meet them and dive beneath when they break. Above all, don't panic. People often as not drown themselves, Dad felt, by failing to remain calm.

My father's aquatic sensibilities, as much as anything else, define a particular aspect of his character that is often overlooked. They are the flip side of the dogged, head-butting stubbornness he brought to his youthful football endeavors and his truculence regarding certain ideological positions in his later political career. In many ways they reflect the nature of that hidden 10 percent he kept largely under wraps — watchful, flexible, isolated. While often seeming — in public, anyway — to have his feet set in stone, Dad was actually surprisingly good at catching waves and evading obstacles with a bit of deft compromise.

Not everyone brought such fluid calm to the Rock River, of course. Rivers are tricky enough as it is; add people seemingly determined to drown themselves, maybe throw in a bit of illicit moonshine, and conditions get exponentially more treacherous.

By late August, with the harvest coming to an end, men and boys from the surrounding farm country would begin showing up at

Lowell Park in greater numbers. These "big strapping fellas," as Dad remembered them to me, might have been all muscle, but that didn't mean they knew how to stay afloat. Ensnared by invisible liquid tentacles, they would be drawn into the main current and begin to flounder. A drowning man doesn't have much of an ear for reason, and fear will turn him into a lethal threat. My father told me he would rarely approach a victim head on, as it was safer to dive beneath and come upon them from behind. He would, on occasion, when facing a frantic, wildly clawing victim, employ a technique they may not have covered at the Y's lifeguard program: a right cross to the jaw.

Dad confessed to feeling real dread only once. A massive hulk of a man, completely blind, arrived at the beach one afternoon. How on earth, Dutch wondered, would he be able to perform a rescue should such a man get into trouble and begin fighting for his life? Forget about a punch in the mouth — you'd need a baseball bat to subdue someone so enormous. Sure enough, out into the water paddled the sightless giant where, within minutes, he became disoriented and was swept into the middle of the river. A cry of alarm went up from the crowd of onlookers as the poor fellow panicked, rearing up vertically, beating ineffectually at the surface with his huge hands. Dutch was already in the water, stroking out to intercept him. As he followed the man's bobbing head down-river, it occurred to him that this might be his last rescue attempt. Many drowning victims scratch and grab, but if a man this size was to latch onto his rescuer, he could easily drag him to the bottom. Dutch imagined the two of them locked in a hideous embrace, tumbling over Dixon's dam and rolling along the riverbed all the way to Sterling, the next town downstream. To his great relief, though, when he reached the man and put a hand on him, the reaction was immediate and total compliance. Accustomed to being guided his entire life, this man had come to associate human touch with safety and security. He instantly relaxed once he felt someone alongside him. "Turned out to be one of my easiest rescues," Dad told me. And a lesson in the vagaries of human nature: The man gave one of the few thanks Dutch ever received.

"One summer, a coach for the Olympic team offered me a place at the swimmers' training camp." My father waited until I was in my early thirties to drop this little nugget of historical clarification into one of our conversations. It came out of nowhere as we were sitting poolside at the Bel Air home my parents had bought just before moving back from Washington, D.C. I'd never heard of any such offer before that moment, and it appears in neither of Dad's autobiographies. "Excuse me? Did you say the Olympic training camp?" He was full of surprises, that father of mine. "Yup," he answered, but didn't seem inclined to elaborate. Not for a moment did I think he would fabricate such a thing. Editing unpleasantness from his life story, confusing movie plots with historical exploits, sure. Making stuff up out of whole cloth in a demented attempt to self-aggrandize, never. "Well . . . what did you tell him?" I asked, still reeling at the thought of my own father as a potential Olympian. "Told him, 'No thanks.' Couldn't afford to give up my lifeguarding job. The money was too important."

Though Dad didn't specify, he must have been talking about the 1932 Olympic Games. Buster Crabbe, just three years older than my father and the heir apparent to Johnny Weissmuller, starred for the men, taking gold in the 400-meter freestyle. He then headed off to Hollywood — cue the score signaling ironic coincidence! — eventually playing Tarzan and Flash Gordon. Had he managed to make the team, Dad may have been able to do his country a solid service — and not just by replacing Crabbe in a series of low-budget serials. America's male swimmers were badly outclassed by the Japanese team that year. Crabbe's medal was their only gold.

So, how did an Olympic coach come to stumble across Dutch Reagan, anyway?

My father's college, Eureka, had a swim team — a small one of just four members, if their only yearbook photo is any indication. That is, they had one after my father got it started and dragooned a few buddies to join. He also served as coach, captain, and, no surprise, the team's best swimmer. Dad may have been merely adequate when it came to his first love, football, but he was genuinely talented in the water. His tall, slim frame, well knitted with long, smooth sinew, was ill suited to his duties as a gridiron lineman. Moving through the water, though, he was a hydrodynamic blade. His dim eyesight, which so limited him in other sports, proved no obstacle in an aquatic environment, where blurriness is a common denominator.

That same edition of the *Eureka Pegasus* contains the only record I've found of Dad's competitive swimming career: In the Little 19 (Eureka's sports conference) swimming meet held at Saint Victor on March 22, Dutch Reagan was entered in the 220-, 100-, and 50-yard swims. He scratched the 100-yard entry, qualified in the other two events, and got two fourths in the finals. Four records set. Marks could not be bettered in any college conference in the country.

More than a hint of pride is revealed in that last sentence. The Little 19 may not have been as prestigious as the Big 10, but in the 1920s, athletic talent was spread more equitably among college institutions. Tiny Eureka was expected to hold its own against much larger schools, like Wesleyan, Bradley, and Northern Illinois. Dad's fourth-place results in the conference championships as an inexperienced 19-year-old sophomore were more than creditable. He would hardly have been slower two years later as a senior. By that time, if an Olympic scout was casting a wide net for the top college swimmers in the country, it would not have been surprising to find Dutch Reagan's name on his list.

Naturally, my father and I raced each other up and down the pool throughout my childhood years. By the age of six or seven, I was challenging him. He had a philosophy about our swimming races (or athletic contests of any kind) that involved never letting me win.

He reasoned that once beyond toddlerhood I'd be smart enough to know if he was faking it. This would, in turn, undermine my confidence in a legitimate victory achieved at an older age. Some might find this approach a tad hard-ass. I never took it that way. As a child, I didn't race him expecting to win. I did it for the joy of participating with him in something we both loved. It wasn't as if he swam as fast as he could and left me floundering in his wake; he would make it fun, slowing down to encourage me, pretending the race was actually close, waiting until I'd almost reached the wall before touching home himself. He must have known that one day I would best him in a swimming contest, but he probably imagined it would take place when I was a strapping college lad — perhaps a member of the swim team — finally getting the best of his nearly 70-year-old dad. We were both surprised when it didn't turn out that way.

The summer of my twelfth year was something of an interlude, if not quite an idyll. During each of the previous three summers, I had spent a solid month away at a wilderness camp in Colorado, rafting, riding, and discovering that grass snakes do not particularly appreciate being handled by small boys. The following year I would take the first of a series of summer jobs, bucking hay and rounding up horses at a dude ranch. But during this twelfth summer, I was largely at liberty.

Much of my time, sweltering through a Sacramento summer, was spent in the water. I had joined the local swim club the year before and performed without distinction at the bottom of my age group. Something about the individual competition, combined with the crowds of onlookers (and quite possibly the alarmingly flamboyant pink paisley Speedos we were forced to wear), made it impossible for me to do the one thing absolutely crucial to a successful swim: relax. The single time Dad came to watch me race, I stood on the starting block, shivering, my prepubescent junk shriveled to a winkle inside my hey-look-me-over trunks, and heard my name announced over the loudspeaker. A hundred heads swiveled from me to my father and back again. When the starter's pistol fired, I hit the water like a box full of rocks.

I'd learned a few useful tricks, though, during my otherwise desultory swim season. One was the flip turn. Most swimmers, casually assaying a few laps in the pool, will, upon reaching the side, grab hold of it and pull their legs underneath them in order to push off for the return trip. Competitive swimmers, you might have noticed while watching the Olympics, instead roll into a forward flip several feet before reaching the wall — a demanding yet considerably more efficient way to execute a turn. Alone in the privacy of the family pool, between games of Marco Polo with playmates and solo reenactments of *Sea Hunt* episodes at the bottom of the deep end, I had been working on my flip turn.

I'm not sure who suggested a race that morning; it wouldn't have been unusual for either of us. These swims were a regular feature of my summers together with Dad. There was nothing forced about them. While he wasn't inclined to throw races to plump up my self-esteem, neither was he the sort of father who enjoyed rubbing his son's nose in a defeat that was a foregone conclusion. A couple or three races a season sufficed.

We both knew how this one would turn out — just like all our previous races: We'd go down and back — two laps. Dad might let up a bit near the finish to make it close; then it would be time for lunch. Never any hard feelings. Just a bit of spirited fun.

Dad and I lined up on opposite sides of the shallow end. My mother stood on the steps between and sent us off with, "On your marks . . . Get set . . . Go!" Down the length of the pool we went, contentedly splashing along in our bubbling, foaming, synchronized submarine solitudes.

While we would both, now and again, utilize a backstroke or breaststroke for fun (neither of us ever got the hang of the butterfly), Dad and I were freestylers by nature, happiest employing the stroke once called the Australian crawl. This stroke, so familiar now, was relatively new to competition at the time Dutch Reagan was born. (Some versions of the crawl, employing various kicks, has probably been used since antiquity; the British eschewed it during the nineteenth century, finding the unavoidable splashing it involved uncivilized.) The first Olympic gold medal won swimming a freestyle that would be recognizable today went to Hawaii's Duke Kahanamoku in 1912. When approached by that Olympic scout as a college competitor, Dad would have been using a stroke developed and disseminated, to a significant extent, during his lifetime.

How did he learn to swim? I never asked and he never mentioned it. He earned some notice swimming at the Dixon Y, of course. But references in his autobiographies and that picture I'd seen in Tampico — nine-year-old Dutch tracking puddles onto the tiny dock at the Hennepin Canal — suggest he was already a budding waterman by the time he reached his hometown on the Rock River. So, who taught him? My guess is his father, Jack, who, once again, may have been left on the cutting-room floor.

Whoever his teacher was, he did a masterful job. Or maybe my father was simply blessed by genetics. Not out of mere filial pride do I say that Dad had one of the most graceful and efficient swimming strokes I've seen this side of Mark Spitz. As a child, I would marvel that he moved as fast as he did without any apparent effort. The instant his fingertips left the water, his recovering arm, instead of describing a circuitous arc on its way back to slapping the surface, would lance forward like a rattlesnake's strike, knifing into the water at a shallow angle and seeming to pull Dad's body along with it. There was very little splash. Extraneous motion was reduced to a minimum. When he rolled his head to take a breath, his mouth barely cleared the waterline. Training aside, he was a natural.

The summer of this particular race, my father and I had both reached ages fraught with peril and uncertainty. For me, at 12, adolescence loomed. Approaching 60, Dad was beginning to pick up the distant strains of mortality's dirge. I don't suppose any of that was on his mind, though, as we headed into our turns at the far end of the pool.

About four feet from the side, I employed my not-so-secret weapon, ducking my head and rolling into an underwater somersault. Till that point in our race, Dad and I had been swimming neck and neck. This in itself was a bit surprising, but I wasn't letting it distract me. Even with practice, flip turns were a crapshoot, and I could execute a decent one in only half my attempts. On this morning luck was with me. As I flipped over and planted my feet squarely on the wall, gathering myself for the home stretch, I glanced across the pool to see Dad just reaching for the side. I pushed off, head down between my shoulders, arms reaching ahead, body held taut and as arrow-straight as possible, lancing toward the far end until my momentum slowed, then pulling hard with my right arm, and rolling sideways to take a deep draw of air. Another quick look to my left told me I had gained a full body length on my father.

Dad, completing his own old-style turn, must have felt a spike of adrenaline pulsing through his body upon finding himself suddenly behind. When was the last time he had lost a swimming race? Looking back as

I moved down the pool, I could see a cloud of froth blooming at his heels as he began kicking furiously, trying to make up lost distance, but to no avail. A few yards from the finish, I knew I would win. Lengthening my stroke, I pulled as strongly as I could and glided to the wall. Raising my head from the water, I looked across the pool just in time to see my father finish.

My mother had been waiting at the end of the pool, ready to deliver the usual consolation speech to her vanquished son: *It was a close race; you're getting faster all the time; maybe next year.* Now, breathing hard through my victor's grin, I saw a look cross her face that was unfamiliar: one of pleasure in my triumph, to be sure, but one that also contained something very much like sadness. Dad caught it, too. He didn't have to ask.

"Well, whattaya know?" he offered, his voice soft and quizzical as he turned to regard his beaming young son. "Congratulations. That was a good swim."

I can't claim that this swimming race was a life-changing moment akin to finding one's father soused and unconscious on the front stoop. But these Oedipal watersheds turn the keys to adulthood nonetheless. The child rises; the father declines.

The dad who could whip all other dads is brought low, so that his son can take his place among the world of men. An old story, and one that, at age 12, I was in no measure ready to complete. For Dad, the unexpected loss must have raised more complex emotions. My mother surely recognized this. As I went back to frolicking in the deep end and my father climbed slowly out of the pool, I watched as she approached with a towel and draped it tenderly over his shoulders.

Summer was coming to an end. Neither Dad nor I sought a rematch. By the following year, he would be 60. I would be a teenager — a bit taller, incrementally stronger, and, we both understood, out of reach. The days when I would happily, hopelessly challenge my athletic father's prowess in the water were over. We never raced again.

Dad wasn't quite ready to let my victory go, however. He mulled things over and, later that night, over dinner, turned to me with a question. "Say, did you do one of those flip turns?" While being careful not to in any way diminish my accomplishment, he was appending an asterisk to my triumph. I had won fair and square — there could be no disputing that — but only through the use of a technique unpracticed in his day.

Dad had found a way to turn his unexpected defeat into a win for both of us.

Lifeguarding is a solitary profession. You might be perched on a high chair for all the beachgoers to gaze at, you might interact reassuringly with the public, but the work itself requires a certain aloofness. You watch; you patiently wait; you study people and their habits; you observe the river until you can gauge its temper. Friends and admirers may stop by to chat, but they will understand if you seem lost in thought, distracted by weightier matters. They know that when trouble arises, the consequences of calamity will fall on your shoulders. You can't afford to become overly sentimental about the folks under your care, though you will risk your life to save any one of theirs. The river is a great leveler: bankers, farmers, shopkeeper's wives — all can be reduced, with shocking suddenness, to notches on your log. You alone are at the center. In your hands rest tranquility and order. You are the Protector.

Sounds like the perfect job for Ronald Wilson Reagan.

Devoted schoolboy essayist that he was, Dutch naturally plumbed his lifeguarding experiences for material, helpfully providing a scattering of clues as to the mind-set he carried through those long-ago summer days.

A piece about a canoeist caught in a summer storm, entitled "Squall," while having little to do with his own professional responsibilities, demonstrates in vigorous language, nevertheless, a keen eye for the volatile mix of natural elements Dutch encountered on the Rock River:

[L]ike an avenging pack the wind is upon you, battering, pulling the paddle from your grasp, screaming in your ears. The whitecaps fling themselves up under your prow, up — up you hang motionless then down with sickening speed, crashing into the next wave with a shuddering blow that racks every rib.

Dutch, it appears, has an appreciative eye as well for his own physical beauty — another essay mentions approvingly a certain lifeguard's "broad chest" and "long, tan legs." As for potential victims, a story published in the *Dixonian* his senior year, "Meditations of a Lifeguard," reduces them, first, to an abstract horde: "A mob of water-seeking humans intent on giving the beach guard something to worry about." Singly, they become typecast: "A big hippopotamus with a

sandwich in each hand, and some firewater
tanked away in his business man's addition.
He'll need watching." With the solipsism
of adolescence, he has turned subjects into
objects.

Of course, Dutch is a teenage boy. Some
objects are rewarded with extra scrutiny:

[S]he's walking onto the dock now. She
trips gracefully over to the edge of the
crowded pier, and settles like a butterfly.
The lifeguard strolls by, turns and strolls
by again. Then he settles in the immediate region of the cause of all this sudden
awakening. He assumes a manly worried
expression, designed to touch the heart
of any blonde, brunette, or unclassified
female. He has done all that's necessary.

Who could ask for more? A bit of a walk
by atop those "long, tan legs" — giving her
a chance to take in the manly swimmer's
pectorals — then, deployment of the pen-
sive, faraway expression. Let her come to
you. My father — who, after all, had been an
object of his mother, Nelle's, adoration his
entire life — liked to be courted. Whether in
politics or love — anywhere his natural role
would be that of suitor — Dad would often
play hard to get. However smitten or ambi-

tious he might be, he was uncomfortable as the pursuer. He wanted to be wooed.

Not long ago, my mother told me about a conversation she'd had, after she and Dad had been seeing each other for some time, with Nelle Reagan. "One day, when we'd been dating a while," she said, "Nelle pulled me aside. She asked me, 'You're in love with him, aren't you?' I told her, 'Yes, I am.' She looked at me and said, 'You'll have to be patient.'"

As a potential candidate for the governorship of California, Dad told his advisers (and his family) he would only consider a run once he had gone on the road, delivered a few speeches, and gauged the enthusiasm of "the people" for his candidacy. Were they sufficiently rapturous, he'd be good to go. If not . . . well, that was something he didn't dwell on. Of course, he was already determined to run; he remained uncomfortable, though, as he had always been, proclaiming grandiose ambition or seeming overeager. Even at a tender age I think I grasped that we were all indulging him in something of a charade in this regard. It was hard to imagine what level of hostility, or how many episodes of ripe fruit throwing, could possibly have dissuaded my father from any campaign he had decided, in his own mind, to mount. Yet it was equally obvious that any forthright display of naked ambition was out of the question.

Aside from Bee Frey's photos and a tiny handful of scattered snapshots, there are few images of my father as a lifeguard at Lowell Park. Some years back, however, producers at PBS, putting together a documentary about my father's life, unearthed an astonishing four minutes of film shot sometime during the late 1920s or early 1930s featuring him cavorting on the Rock River.

Photographs of our parents in their youth are always intriguing: How curious to see them as babies, kids, teenagers; to see them, in any case, before we arrived. Moving images on film are another experience altogether, especially images this old. Around eighty years ago, someone lugged a heavy motion picture camera and tripod down to the beach at Lowell Park. It was an obvious locale to record action, not to mention a venue for scantily clad (all things being relative) young women. Who do you suppose supplied the action that captured the cameraperson's eye?

After lingering for a moment over some children at play on the river's pebbly shore, the camera finds Dutch, tall and square in

219

his singlet. Did he offer to demonstrate a few dives on film or, knowing that a cinematographer would be drawn to motion, did he simply begin launching himself off the high board built onto the dock and let nature take its course?

There he is, lithe and flat-bellied in grainy black and white. Judging by his size, I'd say he's beyond his midteens, probably between 18 and 20. Details are fuzzy, owing to the age and quality of the film; at a distance, Dutch's face is indistinct. But his movements are uncannily familiar: the way he sets himself before each dive; the attitude of his arms and bouncing stride as he moves down the board; his swimming stroke as he returns to the platform; the dives themselves — swans, jackknives, cutaways. All are immediately recognizable to me after years absorbing them along with the chlorinated water in my family's backyard pool.

Having attracted a small coterie of female admirers, Dutch next repairs to the waterslide. There, over the very waters that separated Gus Whiffleberg from his dental plate, our young lifeguard demonstrates his agility, sliding down feet first before rotating into a headfirst dive as he shoots off the lip.

For his grand finale, Dutch climbs the ladder of the slide, maybe 15 feet above the water, to execute a series of dives. Gracefully, boldly, he flings himself into space. But he overrotates on each attempt, sending a plume of spray arcing toward the middle of the river.

Dutch has been playing to the camera all along. His body language during his diving display — at least to someone who knows him intimately — reveals self-consciousness. Later, though, the filmmaker appears to catch him unawares. In shallows no more than thigh-deep, sheltered by the dock, he is giving a swimming lesson to a little boy. Gently he draws the boy, sputtering and kicking, through the placid water, all the while glancing up now and again to take in the rest of the scene. Dad had a particular way of scratching his nose when his allergies acted up — just a reflexive swipe that was peculiarly his own. Watching as Dutch releases his pupil's hands for a moment, I hear myself suck in a sharp breath. There it is: the swipe — unconscious, unaltered, identical. How is it that such a small gesture can be so enduring? Or perhaps it is just such nuances — an arch of the brow, a tip of the head — that become our most durable legacies. Will people, long after they've forgotten his tax cuts and tax increases, even his role in ending the Cold War, still remember the way Ronald Reagan nodded and winked?

Just before the film clip ends, with Dutch continuing his swimming lesson, I watch as he reaches down — idly, with unforced affection — to give the small boy's hair a friendly tousle. Though I don't quite know why, I feel my eyes begin to sting.

I return to Lowell Park a couple of days after my first ill-fated venture, this time in broad daylight. The beach remains nearly deserted. A couple of kids smoking a joint in the parking lot greet me with false bravado as I pull alongside their car. While still home in Seattle, I had considered the possibility of swimming (or at least swimming in) the Rock River. I even packed a bathing suit. Looking out at the sullen, muddy expanse of water beyond the edge of lawn, I realize how ridiculous that would be. Never mind the bovine effluent that originally closed the beach to swimming or the industrial runoff upstream; still swollen by spring thunderstorms, washing who knows what downstream, the river is plain uninviting. I content myself with a walk along its bank.

Many of the oaks standing on the park's lawn appear to be old enough to have been growing when my father lifeguarded. Which tree might have been the one under which he manned his station, I cannot tell. Near an asphalt boat ramp, a small floating dock slumps, half submerged, in shallow water. This, I know, was the location of the dock, waterslide, and diving board during Dutch's day. This spot was the center of his universe during those hot summers so long ago.

Once again, I call on my imagination to conjure my young father: Here he comes, striding across the lawn in his slightly stiff-legged way — as if his upper body were balanced atop two slim pilings — corralling a gaggle of kids playing too boisterously around the dock. At six feet one inch, he has nearly reached his adult height. There isn't an ounce of excess on his 175-pound frame. As he barks at the boys, I note that his voice is higher than most people suppose, well into the tenor range, with just a hint of nasality — all the pollen blowing around can't be doing those allergies any good. He is strikingly good-looking, with a small, square head set on a short neck and broad, straight shoulders, and he moves with a fluid economy of motion. Having been out of the water awhile, he has taken time to neatly comb his hair, which otherwise tends to go its own way. The hair, while hardly blond, has bleached considerably under the relentless sun. He parts it on the left, opposite to what a Hollywood stylist will later advise. As he turns from chastising the youngsters, a crooked smile lifts the right side of his face. Then, as he continues walking, I see the smile fade, replaced by an inscrutable, faraway look. Someone calls out to him from near the food stand, "Hey, Dutch!" but he seems not to notice. Reaching his lifeguard's chair, he picks up a pair of thick, black-rimmed glasses and slips them on. His face takes on an earnest expression. Leaning forward slightly, he returns to watching the bathers in the water. No one is going to drown on his watch. Not a one.

Dutch exudes an air of much greater assurance now. He is a long way from the undersized tyke picked last for games and chased home by bullies from yet another new school. But the little boy who contentedly dreamed over butterfly wings in the dusty sunbeams of a neighbor's attic remains within, quietly nursing ambitions, steadily assembling the elements of his story. His looks, his ease, his physical prowess — all have combined in some indefinable way to produce that most valuable of commodities: charisma. He is more and more certain of the effect he has on other people but less sure how to turn that to his advantage.

On the banks of the Rock River's Grand

Detour, Dutch Reagan has found a place where the solitary soul he is can comfortably cohabit with the public figure he wants to become. On this stage — admired by women, envied by men — he is the undisputed leading man. Yet he is also alone with his thoughts. Many of those thoughts turn to the role in life he hopes to assume. Much as he enjoys lifeguarding, for all that it has contributed to his sense of self, he is certain that he is cut out for a life of accomplishment far beyond the banks of the Rock River. He has been going to the movies every chance he gets. In the back of his mind, the thought that this relatively new medium might take him places he wants to go has begun to take hold. But Hollywood is a distant realm to a small-town lifeguard from the Midwest. Dutch fantasizes about recognition, stardom, a sense of accomplishment beyond a steady paycheck. But with the country spiraling into the Great Depression, virtually all opportunities are beginning to look like fantasies. So Dutch falls back on a dream of glory much closer to home — the one revealed in that letter he wrote as an 11-year-old. Maybe no one thanks him for having been saved from drowning, but he knows full well how to bring an entire stadium (or at least a couple of rows of bleachers) to its feet. In less than a month, he'll be back on the campus of Eureka for his senior year. Falling leaves, the evocative scent of liniment, the thud of a cleated boot against pigskin — another football season is almost upon him. Surely, on Eureka's field of glory, he will find what he's looking for.

CHAPTER SEVEN
FIELDS OF GLORY

Alzheimer's spared my father many of its typical indignities — unaccountable rages, fits of paranoia, and the like. But as the disease progressed, he was troubled for a time by a persistent delusion. After an afternoon spent quietly watching televised football games in the little den that, more and more, had become the center of his diminishing world, he would awaken in the darkness of the early morning utterly convinced that he needed to suit up and take the field. "There's a game. They're waiting for me," he would tell my mother as he tried to push past her to reach the bedroom door. She would struggle to hold her ground, eventually and with great difficulty talking him back to bed.

As it strips away layers of hard-won synapses, Alzheimer's reduces its victims to their primary elements. My father was not concerned, during those wee-hours fugue states, about being late for a cabinet meeting. The voices in his head were not calling "Lights! Camera! Action!" He was not even in an Iowa radio studio waiting for a ticker tape to alert him to balls and strikes. He had, instead, been transported to a time much nearer the beginning, back to the autumn days of his boyhood. He was once again on the playing fields of Dixon, or maybe Eureka College. Affairs of state, the vagaries of a career in show business, all these had long since been swallowed by the brambles choking his mind's dying garden. He was not afraid of disappointing some studio director or leaving a visiting dignitary waiting. His concerns were those of his youth: He couldn't let down his teammates; they were counting on him. The faces emerging from his shredded consciousness no longer belonged to Mikhail Gorbachev or Jack Warner; they were those of his long-ago gridiron role models: Garland Waggoner, Pebe Leitch, Enos "Bud" Cole, Mac McKinzie. He couldn't be a no-show with the big game on the line. He was ready: ready for the rushing tumult in the chill afternoon; ready for the thrill of being part of it all; ready to show them what he could do — show them that he, too, had the stuff of heroes.

"It's funny," he told me years earlier, "whenever I think of playing football back then, it's always a gray, cloudy day." Now, as his good days dwindled to a few, the disease that would eventually kill him was carrying him back to those gray days.

"I loved three things: drama, politics, and sports, and I'm not sure they always come in that order." I'm not sure they did either. When Dad wrote those words in *Where's the Rest of Me?*, his 1965 autobiography, the intended message was that politics had, by that time, become his principal fixation — he was no longer "just an actor"; the time for youthful fun and games was past. While there is plenty about his already recognizable political philosophy in the book, a reader can't help but notice that his prose seems most engaged and alive when he's recounting (and perhaps somewhat embellishing) athletic trials and triumphs on the playfields of his youth. It is equally apparent that his all-consuming passion is the game of football.

In the 1920s football was already well on its way to becoming a national craze. Though the forward pass had been introduced earlier in the century, the game was still reminiscent of rugby — five yards and a cloud of dust or, more likely, a thumb-in-the-eye pileup in the mud. Leather helmets were used, but there were no face masks; padding was rudimentary. Far from the hypersonic air show we're used to seeing these days, with its constantly shifting lineups of multimillionaire specialists, football 1920s-style was a smash-mouth affair played mostly by burly farm boys and Appalachian sons of the coal. The same players typically lined up on both offense and defense. The dropkick was still a popular weapon. A professional league had been created in 1920, but the attention of most fans, young Dutch included, was riveted on the exploits of college players like Red Grange at the University of Illinois and Notre Dame stars like George Gipp (yes, The Gipper) and the fabled Four Horsemen. These athletes were distant deities to small-town kids like Dad, but there were always heroes to be found closer to home.

Idiosyncratic spelling and punctuation notwithstanding, that letter sent by 11-year-old Dutch to Gladys Shippert and her sister — the one in which he briefly relishes the thought of slaughtering a few rabbits for dinner — leaves little doubt as to where his chief interests lie:

Dixon Highschool has played 10 games won 8 tied 1 and lost 1 they tied sterling. They cant have the thanksgiving game

230

because of the smallpox in Sterling. I play quarterback on the [South Central school] team Sat we were going to play the [North Central school] team but there captain got yellow and he wouldn't play . . . Sat. Dixon went to Rochell and beat them 27 to 6 the game we lost was with dekalb. They beat us 6 to 0.

Note the casual reference to a smallpox outbreak a few miles downriver — a vivid reminder of the era in which my father grew up.

The young women may not have cared how Dixon High, much less my father's elementary school, was faring on the football field, but his mention of a recent Dixon celebrity might have caught their eye: "monday mama got a letter from mrs. Wagnor and she said Garland has made the team at Eureka they played Illinois last week." John Garland Waggoner II had been a football star at Dixon High the year before and had made the varsity team at Eureka College his freshman year. He was something of a local hero and one of Dutch's early idols. Six years later Dad would follow Waggoner to Eureka, hoping to match his feat as a first-year letterman. It would be a great shock to his system and cause him no small amount of misery when he failed.

Eureka was (and remains) a small Christian college some 75 miles south of Dixon. Its association with the Disciples of Christ suggests that Nelle, by this point a prominent figure in Dixon's church community, may have been instrumental in securing her son a spot on campus. On the other hand, with a small enrollment that had been steadily shrinking since the 1880s, the school was probably more than eager to welcome him despite his need for a scholarship. Students numbered about 250 in Dad's day, divided roughly evenly between men and women. To Dutch Reagan, that meant there would be only about 125 aspiring Gippers who could possibly compete for spots on its football team. With this in mind, and noting that the college had just struggled through two consecutive losing seasons, Dutch thought his chances of making the starting roster were pretty good. His timing was as unfortunate as his ego was inflated.

Though blessed with stamina, agility, and molten desire, Dad had a few liabilities that, from high school through college, combined to make him an unlikely football star: his lack of size, less than blazing speed, and fuzzy vision. His extreme nearsightedness put positions like quarterback or wide receiver out of reach once he left grade school — he simply couldn't see balls spiraling through the air or, for that matter, easily distinguish teammates from opponents at a distance of more than a few yards. Wearing his glasses was not an option. Desperate to participate nonetheless, he spent a lot of time competing for a position on the interior line, which meant long afternoons being knocked around by much bigger boys.

A Dixon High team photo from 1924 is almost heartbreaking. There's my freshman father, all five feet three inches and 108 pounds of him, cross-legged on the turf in a row with all the other third-stringers. He is holding his helmet in his hands and looking very much like himself — his thick hair is swept back off his forehead; a crooked smile is spread across his face; he appears utterly content in his own skin. All innocence and eagerness, he clearly can't wait to take the field and impress coaches and teammates alike with his sporting prowess. But closer inspection reveals a little boy swimming in oversized pads. His thin neck looks desperately vulnerable poking up through the manhole of his jersey collar. As he tells it later, there were no pants small enough to fit him. Behind him, double ranked, stand at least 20 reasons why he will spend much of the next couple of frustrating years warming the bench. Among the varsity starters, many of whom look like full-grown men, we find Dutch's brother, Moon. Two years older and the speedster in the family, Moon is the team's starting end. The contrast between the two, as always, is striking, and not just in terms of relative size. While Dutch radiates earnest good-boy vibes — every skinny inch of him Nelle's son — Moon carries himself with an air of wry insouciance. Nearly the biggest member of the team, thick through the chest and shoulders, he looks like a bruiser. He has unstrapped his leather helmet for the photo and wears it cocked at a jaunty angle. In place of his little brother's winning grin, Moon's face wears its usual knowing smirk. He is clearly Jack's boy.

With the help of a summer spent shoveling, hammering, and pushing a wheelbarrow for a local construction crew, Dutch finally grew husky enough by his sophomore year to start for his Dixon High team. He managed to remain on the first string through the rest of his high school career, an accomplishment he elevated in his own mind to sports stardom. Leafing through his Dixon High senior yearbook, I find a more mundane story. The section devoted to Dixon's football season notes that Dutch

Reagan "took care of his tackle berth in a creditable manner" and approvingly mentions his "true 'Dixon' spirit."

The entire scenario would be repeated at Eureka College. Reporting to his first practice scrimmage in the fall of 1928, hair cropped close at the sides but left full and parted down the middle on top — "like the hero of the comic strip *Harold Teen*" — he found himself in the company not just of other eager high school grads, but of seasoned adults. While the Great Depression was not yet officially under way, jobs in farm country had been drying up for some time. Boys who left high school for once abundant employment had been laid off and were now returning to college as men. Prospective teammates like Bud Cole, for instance, had, by the time he reached college, spent three years playing pro ball, lending him, as Dad later put it, "a big-time flavor."

Another team; another team photo: Though Dutch certainly looks beefier as a college scrub than he did as a 14-year-old high school freshman, the rugged lineup flanking him still makes you fear for his safety. The sunny, lopsided smile he usually presents a photographer has been replaced during that first season by a scowl. Of all the Golden Tornadoes (disappointingly, the team has since changed its name to the far less evocative Red Devils) he is the only one not wearing a maroon and gold uniform. He stands amid his properly attired teammates sulking in a frayed white practice jersey. Dutch has convinced himself that he is first-team material, but Eureka's coach clearly has other ideas.

Ralph McKinzie (everyone called him Mac) was one tough plug of shoe leather. An athletic prodigy from Oklahoma, he had followed his high school coach to Eureka a decade before. There he earned varsity letters in football, basketball, and baseball four years running. All-around athlete though he was, his specialty was football. After a game in which he scored all 52 of Eureka's points, a Peoria newspaper headline summed it up: MCKINZIE BEATS BRADLEY 52–0. Following graduation Mac returned to Eureka as its head football coach. He may not have had much else on his mind, but he knew his favorite game inside out. Keen-eyed when it came to athletic horseflesh, he took one look at still gangly Dutch Reagan, caught wind of some of his boasting, and promptly consigned him to the bench.

Mention of my father in the Athletics section of his Eureka yearbook hints at a freshman season distinguished more by effort than accomplishment:

> Although "Dutch" failed to get much competition this season, he has the determination and fight which will finally win out, if he sticks to football throughout his college career. He was shifted about on second string from end to tackle, doing his best wherever he was put. Another thing to Reagan's credit is that he was a regular at all practices, a thing which is pleasing to any coach.

But not quite pleasing enough. Whether McKinzie was moved by pigskin savvy, a tenderhearted concern for keeping a young man in one piece, or simply annoyance that this same cocky kid had been bending everyone's ear with inflated tales of his high school football prowess, he wasn't about to let Dutch into any games. My father took it badly. He was doing his best — never missed a practice! Why wouldn't the coach, a man who, at this juncture, represented everything to which my father aspired, allow him to play? He stewed on the bench all freshman season and then, over the summer, told friends and family that he would not be returning to Eureka. The first person in his family ever to attend college, and he was ready to give it up because his football coach won't show him the recognition he felt he deserved. The fierceness of his drive to stand out — not to mention his intolerance for being thwarted, however justifiably — is evident in this rash impulse. You can also sense his vulnerability when seemingly ignored by a man he looked to as a father figure.

Recounting this period in his autobiographies, Dad will obscure the issue a bit, admitting he felt rejected by his coach, but also bringing up money worries as a relevant factor. He had been receiving a needy-student half scholarship to attend Eureka, washing dishes in his fraternity house to cover his room and board. Funds were tight. A copy of his college loan application, dated 1931, reflects his financial situation: He has $30 in savings, plus $50 in gifts from friends and family, and expects to earn another $75 working during the school year. With a $200 loan he will have $455, leaving him only $37 shy of his projected expenses, which include $90 for tuition and $288 for room and board.

Late that first summer home from college, with autumn approaching, he signs on with a road crew whose foreman was formerly on the rowing team at the University of Wis-

238

consin. The man offers him a deal: Work for one year; I'll get you a rowing scholarship at Wisconsin. "It was an offer too good to refuse," Dad later recalled. But, in the end, he would.

I feel plenty of sympathy for my father. While the expense of tuition was never an issue for me growing up, I can identify with both his athletic frustration and his sense of injustice, however wayward. Though I never played sports in college (I left after one semester at Yale to pursue a career as a professional ballet dancer), I did compete as an undersized schoolboy athlete and — more Moon than Dutch — as an overachieving rule breaker. My first high school — private, boarding, boys only, nestled in the smog-smothered foothills southeast of Los Angeles — had about the same enrollment in the 1970s as Eureka College had had nearly a half century earlier. As at Eureka — where "everybody was needed," as my father put it — my school encouraged students to pitch in. I did triple duty, filling out the jock, stoner, and arts cliques, as well as keeping busy with extracurricular activities like class cutting and pranks. My teachers mostly seemed baffled that the score on my IQ test wasn't being reflected in my schoolwork.

Between my second and third years, I was mortified, upon returning home one July afternoon, to find the principal and dean of students sitting in my parents' living room. My grades were mostly Bs, though I pulled some Cs, and even an occasional D, in classes like algebra and French, which I more or less ignored. I hadn't actually been caught committing any violation worthy of suspension or expulsion, yet here were these school officials telling my parents I was a trouble-maker, leading other kids astray. I would enter my junior year on probation — one slip and I was out. Though my father's ears pricked up when the principal mentioned the "leadership qualities" I presumably used to practice my malign voodoo, the thrust of this presentation was obviously nothing my parents wanted to hear. Still, it was some-thing they seemed distressingly eager to accept, as principal and dean met with no skepticism. There were no pointed questions about just what I had done to deserve such a rap, but instead, everyone took turns glaring at me as if I'd been apprehended in flagrante with the school mascot. From my perspec-tive, this was all a blatant transgression of the rules of the game. Certainly I was engaged in various activities that arguably qualified me as a "bad influence," as the dean kept intoning — you might think of me as a kind of ur–Ferris Bueller. But I wasn't a bad kid — not cruel, not a bully. How could I be punished if all they could come up with was some vague insinuation about enticing fellow students into misbehaving? Fair was fair, and this plainly wasn't. They were just upset that in the contest of, I break the rules and you try to catch me, I was winning. As being benched by Coach Mac had to my father, the whole thing seemed monstrously unjust. Besides, hadn't I been faithfully representing my school on the sports field? Didn't that count for something?

While soccer was, by my day, a viable option for the student athlete, it was still considered a bit of a cop-out among most of my jock friends. As in my father's era, tough guys played football, even if they stood only five feet four inches and weighed in at a burly 120 pounds with a full book bag. But on a freshmen/sophomore team desperate for bodies, I was just fleet and gritty enough to crack the starting lineup. Of course, holding my own against friends and teammates was one thing; it was another matter altogether when it came to those Saturday afternoon games against total strangers who always seemed to have emerged from some foundry for the extra-large. During my sophomore year someone got the bright idea of matching our little team of overprivileged underclassmen against a much larger public school's junior varsity. On the appointed day, as the 25 or so of us went about our pregame warm-up on a neutral field, the opposing JVs arrived on a large chartered bus, raucously disgorging in what seemed to be their hundreds like some Visigoth horde. Many, if not most, appeared to weigh over 200 pounds. I looked around at my skinny, long-haired teammates and thought to myself, *This is not going to go well*. It didn't. I don't remember the final embarrassing score, nor do I recall when the rival coach mercifully began playing his third string. I believe his eight-year-old daughter might have taken a few snaps at quarterback, but I can't be sure. I was a bit disoriented by then. I do remember angling out into the flat as a receiver on one of our invariably desperate third-down plays and foolishly making the mistake of catching the ball. This only seemed to provoke the terrifyingly immense defenders. While one lunged low, tying up my legs and rendering me immobile, another pounded forward to deliver a forearm shot to my face, splitting my mouth guard in half and leaving my helmet perched on the back of my head like a yarmulke. Back in the huddle, spitting blood, I wryly suggested that it was still not too late to make a break for the parking lot.

I suspect Dutch Reagan would have chastised me for my lack of school spirit.

For the record, midway through my junior year — bloodshed on the school's behalf apparently inconsequential — I was told I would no longer be welcome at the aforementioned institution, having been given the boot over a technical infraction too tedious to recount.

In one of those moments of serendipity that seemed to follow my father through life (or, at least, life as he later recounted it), his first day of work with the road crew is canceled due to a pelting rainstorm. He calls his girlfriend, Mugs Cleaver, who, as it happens, is about to drive back to Eureka with her parents. Having nothing better to do, Dutch catches a ride with them, "just for a visit." While there, he pays a call on his ostensible nemesis, Coach McKinzie, and informs him the football squad will be a man short that coming fall. Mac then gives him the opening he desperately wants by expressing disappointment that he'll be losing a member of the team. This is obviously just what my father wants to hear. The clouds lift, and raindrops are replaced by welcoming rays of autumn sunshine. His coach needs him after all. In his later telling, Dutch "falls in love with Eureka all over again." Next thing you know, Mac — now newly adorned in the raiment of benevolent wisdom — is visiting school officials to line up another partial scholarship (the remaining costs deferred till after graduation) for him and finding him a job washing dishes in the girls' dorm to cover his expenses. Nelle is phoned and told to send his belongings. Just like that, Dutch is back at Eureka.

Missing from Dad's later accounts is any mention of how his initial decision to skip a year of college was greeted back home. Jack and Moon, who both saw higher education as an unnecessary diversion from getting on in the world, may have felt some smug satisfaction. Nelle, on the other hand, who always envisioned big things for her younger son, can't have been pleased, and she was not one to hide her displeasure. There must have been some awkward nights around the dinner table, willful Dutch being made to feel he was a disappointment, particularly to the tiny, strong-jawed woman who was still the most dynamic force in his life.

We also get no sense of how his soon-to-be fiancée, Mugs, whom he had followed to Eureka, felt about his impulsive move, though she was likely as disappointed as Nelle. Mugs was counting on better than a college dropout. What stands out in this incident is that, in a fit of adolescent pique, my father was willing to jeopardize not only his best shot at a college degree, but his relationship with his first love as well.

At the center of his personal narrative, at this early stage, was college football fame. It was a fixation that filled his waking fantasies. Frustrated that obdurate reality would not allow itself to be easily molded to suit his needs, and lacking the emotional maturity to modify those needs to conform to life as he found it, he reacted first with anger and self-pity: It can't be that I'm simply not good enough for the first string; some illegitimate personal vendetta on the part of my coach must be to blame. He would have to pursue his dream elsewhere, somewhere his manifest talents would be appreciated. In other words, he was thinking and acting like a headstrong, self-absorbed teenager.

I suspect, though, that he was never really comfortable with his plan to abandon Eureka or its football team. The college's ivied brick halls matched perfectly his youthful vision of what a college should be, and his private, more calculating side must have realized that failing to make the starting

245

squad at tiny Eureka didn't bode well for his chances at a major university. No, leaving school must have seemed a bigger and bigger mistake as summer wore on. Not least, it would paint him as a quitter, a decidedly unheroic label that would leave a sour taste in his mouth. He may have returned home full of aggrieved bluster after that first disappointing year, talked himself into a corner, then almost immediately regretted it. He probably spent the whole summer brooding at his lifeguard post on the Rock River, desperately trying to figure out a face-saving means to undo his decision. I don't know what conversation ensued during that drive back to Eureka with Mugs and her father, the formidable Pastor Cleaver — you can easily imagine their efforts at persuasion — but my guess is that my father was already looking for a way back when he climbed into their car, may, in fact, have already amended his internal narrative to accommodate a change of heart. The rain was a lucky break. Coach Mac was just being nice. Stubborn and disinclined as he was to admit mistakes or failure, Dad would, nevertheless, usually find a way, throughout his life, to avoid utter catastrophe by means of an adept script revision. So, he "fell in love" with his college for a second time. And who can argue with affairs of the heart?

You may be thinking that I'm making far too much of my father's football infatuation. But it was his obsession. By his own admission, the chance to play college ball was his primary motivation for attending Eureka in the first place. In retrospect, it seems a bit delusional, but my father pursued his quixotic dream in dead earnest. Football glory seemed the clearest avenue to the acclaim Dutch craved. To this isolated, naive midwestern boy, nothing else at hand seemed to offer as much promise.

At the time, football was seen, by its practitioners and fans, as more than just a game. In the twenties and thirties the gridiron was considered — by wide-eyed fans like my father, at least — a field on which the nation's male youth might test their manhood, a moral crucible, a domestic stand-in for the theater of war, an opportunity for young men to earn a red badge of courage. Quitting was the ultimate failure and branded the offender a coward. The player who abandoned his team lost more than a chance to win a school letter. He betrayed his alma mater, his coach, and his teammates. Most important, in his character lapse he failed himself. Dutch Reagan had already absorbed these lessons by the time he reached Eureka. An avid schoolboy essayist, he often considered in his early writings the perceived moral challenges of his favorite sport. A piece from his high school yearbook, written during his senior year and portentously entitled "Gethsemane," captures the mood. We join the story in progress as . . .

[a]n early harvest moon made ghostly figures of the milky mist tendrils that hung over the deserted gridiron like spirits of long dead heroes, hovering over scenes of ancient triumphs. The level field was silent and lonely to all save the huddled figure who lay stretched out on the close-cropped grass. But to this boy the field was crowded with ghosts of former stars.

Great linemen, brilliant backs who had given their all for the high school were pointing ghostly scornful fingers at him. The quitter cringed before the visions his tortured mind brought up.

What strikes me immediately is that this is impressive work for an 18-year-old. With its stress on action words and arresting images, it reflects the influence of famed sportswriter Grantland Rice. But who is this quitter and what has he done to torture himself so?

The quitter was the greatest half-back the school had ever produced, he was a story book type, tall, good looking and popular. . . .

"Tall, good looking and popular" — sound like anyone we know? So, what could have gone wrong?

Crippled by ineligibility his team had run into competition harder than was expected. Held scoreless, and held to few gains he had quit — refused to risk his brilliant reputation by being flopped for losses.

Naturally, our fallen hero pays the price for valuing his own needs over those of the team.

His soul was being torn apart and all the petty little egotisms were preying on his mind. He realized his grandstand nature, he saw for the first time how cheap he really was. Great sobs shook him and he writhed before the pitiless conscience that drove him on in his agony of self punishment.

Once we understand that my father's protagonists are always stand-ins for the author,

such self-laceration becomes slightly unnerving. But being a true hero at heart, our
lapsed football star will have an epiphany
that turns everything around.

Then his sobs ceased and he stood up, his
face to the sky, and the ghosts of honored
warriors urged him and drew him from the
low shadows. A love and loyalty took the
place of egotism. His hand strayed to the
purple monogram he wore, and as he
looked at the curving track, at the level
field, he realized he loved them.

All that's left for him is to win back the
trust of the team and ride to the rescue
in their hour of desperation. That's what
heroes do. I'll let young Dutch finish his
story without further interruption (and with
whimsical punctuation intact):

Stubborn pride held him in silence while
his team fought a losing battle in the last
game of the season, he had been a quitter but now some sense of honor kept him
from asking to play. The team filed into
the dressing room at the end of the half,
beaten and discouraged. The strained
silence was broken by a stamping and
shouting in the stands above them. Then

they cried as the opening lines of the old loyalty song boomed across the field, and as the last notes died away, so died stubborn pride. The quitter rose and spoke. In three minutes the team trotted out to warm up, and 11 boys were wiping tears from their eyes as the quitter took his place by the fullback.

To finish the story right, perhaps they ought to win the game, but this is a story of football, of football when the score stands thirteen to nothing against you.

Time and again the quitter pounded around right end in a beautiful ground gaining stride that made the coach want to recite poetry, the rhythm was so even. He didn't scurry like so many open field runners; neither did he push and fight his way, but he sailed, and as he side-stepped a man the rhythm remained unbroken, until, as he hit an inevitable tackler, his bird-like flight changed to a ripping, tearing smash that gained a last yard every time.

The game ended a tie. The first score was made when he sprinted thirty seven yards over tackle for a touchdown, after running and smashing his way the length of the field in three short snappy plays. As they carried him off the field he received the perfect tribute; with rooters for both sides standing while waves of sound broke on the gray cloudy sky, broke and seemed to shriek in the ears of the quitter.

And when a friend asked the coach whether he considered the past season successful or not, he thought of the greatest half-back and murmured to himself, "It matters not that you won or lost, but how you played the game."

It's hard to imagine an 18-year-old writing a similar essay today. The fevered emotional pitch might be timeless, but the grim, existential weight attached to a single lapse on the football field — not to mention the fervid declaration of school spirit — would doubtless strike most of the Facebook generation as considerably over the top. Even my father's own peers might have found it nearly as corny.

In any case, virtually all the elements of Dad's private narrative are on display: moral crisis; awakened conscience; selfless hero triumphant. There is a sense, too, of our hero as solitary and separate, even while part of a team. Other contradictions are present as well. The hero conquers petty egoism, only to be rewarded with the "perfect tribute" — all the more satisfying because he not only gains the adulation of his hometown crowd but manages to win over the opposition fans as well. His moral journey, his sterling character forged in the fires of disgrace and redemption, are presumed to be apparent to all in his "ground gaining stride," his "ripping, tearing smash" around right end. His glory is self-evident; he is a hero by virtue of universal acclamation. At the end of the day, even his opponents have become devoted acolytes. (My father was never comfortable with the idea that he might have intractable enemies.) And let's not forget how "tall" and "good looking" he is.

"Why," asks my wife, "do your memories of your father always involve something to do with sports, something physical?" The question leaves me stammering for a reply. She's right, as usual. Ask me for an anecdote about Dad and something sports-related or athletic inevitably rises to the top of the pile. But why?

A more common question: What was it like growing up with a father who was (take your pick) a reasonably famous actor and television host, governor of California, president of the United States? Answer: crowded. When you reach a certain level of celebrity, in whatever field, people begin to think of you as public property. Private as he was in many respects, my father seemed, from his children's jealous perspective, to be alarmingly accepting of that. In fact, he sometimes seemed more comfortable in front of a crowd of total strangers than he did sitting at the dinner table surrounded by family. And why not? While an anonymous audience could usually be counted on for nothing but rapt attention and enthusiastic applause, family frequently made for a tougher room altogether. "How sharper than a serpent's tooth are the words of an ungrateful child," he would frequently intone, misquoting Shakespeare's Lear, whenever any of us took issue with one of his positions.

A big-time political career also means an accretion of staff and advisers. I was seven when Dad began his run for the governorship, and I couldn't help noticing a lot of new people elbowing their way into the family picture. At that age I took a healthily proprietary attitude toward my parents. Though willing to volunteer my father for front-yard touch football games with school friends, I was not inclined to share him with just anyone. But here he was, surrounded by new faces murmuring compliments and impressing him with their grasp of state politics, legislative strategy, and budgetary matters — an array of topics seven-year-olds the world over can be counted on to find skull-crushingly dull. Some of these intruders, like Nancy Reynolds, were the kind of fiercely loyal women who seem peculiarly drawn to politicians. Others, like Lyn Nofziger, were gimlet-eyed campaign pros. Then there were the even closer confidants: Mike Deaver, for instance, became something of an honorary family member. These folks got to spend all day with my father. He seemed to like and respect them. Worse, they became necessary to him in ways I couldn't match. But I had a trump card, an answer — in my own mind, at least — for the adoring crowds and hovering posse.

During those long summer afternoons spent in the family pool, Dad and I used to play a game we called Riding the Whale to the Bottom of the Ocean. As I've mentioned, Dad was fond of swimming laps as a means of staying fit. Back and forth he would go as the summer wore on, stroke after deceptively efficient stroke. After a few laps I would begin pestering him for a ride and, after a few more, he would give in, letting me climb up on his back, the two of us greasy-slick and redolent of Coppertone. Another lap or two across the pool and it would be time for the much anticipated finale. "Ready to ride the whale?" he would call. Then down he'd dive toward the ribbons of light waving over the bottom, with me, a delighted, bubbling Ahab aboard for the descent.

These new arrivals — as a kid I always thought of them as suspiciously pallid "indoor people" — never got to ride the whale. Nor did they share our secret football plays, weekend horseback rides, or body-surfing adventures. His sporting, physical realm was territory I staked out for myself. My mother, of course, could claim her own intimacy. My sister, Patti, to be sure, was my father's most eager equestrian partner. My eldest siblings from my father's first marriage, Maureen and Michael, seemed determined to outdo him at being politically conservative. But the fellow athlete's intuitive sense of a competitor's mass and momentum, strengths and limitations, the sure instinct for angle and trajectory, that particular ligament-and-tendon closeness was something I considered my special purview.

Captured on a snippet of eight-millimeter film — though curiously missing from the copy on hand at the Reagan Library — is a moment from a trip my family took overseas in 1969, my father having been dispatched by President Nixon as some sort of envoy. Beginning with a hopscotching traverse of the Pacific aboard a windowless Air Force

Two, this tour would include rides in open-sided Huey gunships over wartime Saigon, a meet and greet with Chiang Kai-shek and Madame Chiang of Taiwan, and a bout of food poisoning in South Korea. We were also, during one stop, guests of the kleptocratic Philippine dictator, Ferdinand Marcos, and his shoe-fetishist wife, Imelda. Amid a landscape of want, we stayed in the obscenely lavish Malacañang Palace. The walls of my guest quarters, I recall, were covered in mother-of-pearl. To my squirming embarrassment, I was assigned my own personal valet, who hung around outside my bedroom door all night. During a lavish dinner held on the second night of our stay, Marcos's son, a boy about my age who went by the name of Bong-Bong, informed me that my room was haunted. A ghost, he assured me, would knock on my door in the early morning hours. Sure enough, the next day, just as the sky was beginning to lighten, came a soft rapping. It persisted, on and off, until, as dawn broke, I summoned the courage to toss off my blankets and rush to the door. Of course, there was no one there. The ghost may have been reliably knocking pipes, but I've always suspected a mischievous Bong-Bong.

One muggy Philippine morning, as a treat,

we boarded helicopters and flew from Manila to a beach resort for some sun and surf. Unfortunately a cyclone had chosen that moment to spin through our corner of the western Pacific. There was no sun, and the surf was discouraging — a thick, thumping shore break that threatened aquatic mayhem. Naturally my father and I were determined to go swimming. I had by this time spent days cooped up in airplanes and overdecorated rooms, forced to wear nice clothes that made me feel like an impostor. I was desperate to get outside and hurl my body around. Dad, I'm quite sure, felt the same way.

The camera finds him as he's exiting the by then unrideable surf. I'm out of frame wondering how to discreetly dispose of the sand load filling the seat of my bathing suit. Dad strides up the steep coral sand beach, smiling, conscious of being filmed, entirely at ease displaying his 58-year-old body in a pair of brief trunks. At that moment a particularly powerful wave breaks, sending a sheet of water rushing up the incline. With exquisite comedic timing, it catches Dad at the heels just as he's lifting one foot. In a Keystone Kop instant, he is upended and deposited unceremoniously onto his backside. No sooner than he hits the sand do I appear, camera left, dashing knock-kneed to his side. Taking hold of one arm, I dig in my heels and struggle mightily to pull him to his feet. Then, as he gets his legs under him, another wave crashes, and I tear off, 11-year-old courage giving way to an instinct for self-preservation.

Later my mother would tell me, "He was so proud that you came to rescue him." Brushing off the compliment — why couldn't he tell me that himself? — I reminded her I'd been just as quick to beat a retreat. But what was I thinking as I rushed across that beach? Was I afraid he'd been hurt? Concerned he was vulnerable and in danger of being dragged back into the undertow? Did I react to the assault on his dignity? Or was I, once again, planting my flag? I recall to this day the queasy thrill I felt as I lunged forward, matchstick legs churning over that unfamiliar sand, tingling with the excitement of embarking on a course of action the consequence of which I could not predict but which nevertheless seemed unquestionably my responsibility. We had been swimming together, father and son, as we had done countless times. We were a pair, experiencing this beach, this hammering surf, together. The cameraman, staffers, security personnel — as far as I was concerned, all were consigned to a separate realm. They floated in the distance with the other indoor people. They had no standing here. If my father was knocked down, it was my business, my privilege, to pick him up.

After another half season fidgeting on the bench, Dutch Reagan began to turn himself into a serviceable football player. Perhaps his greatest moment of gridiron glory came not in a game but in a practice scrimmage. Obviously proud, Dad devotes considerable attention to this athletic apogee in both of his autobiographies. A recent graduate and former star player had been helping Mac coach the team. One afternoon, as they practiced an end-around play, this fellow lined up on defense as the man my father was meant to block, and he made the mistake of taunting the still second-team pulling guard into full-throttle contact. Dad admits that in no game before or since did he ever hit anyone harder. Old Grad limped off the field; Coach Mac was duly impressed. Soon after, Dutch was elevated to the roster of first-stringers. Better still, here was a legitimate sports anecdote to fit into his life story in the making.

Eureka's yearbook marks his progress, noting that Dutch "never gives up when the odds are against him." His coach stresses the message with one of the few personal inscriptions penned to Dutch that can be found between the *Pegasus* covers, *"Never Give Up! Mac McKinzie."*

Moon also makes an appearance, belatedly, in the yearbook's pages. He had grown disillusioned over the course of three years working a dead-end job at a cement plant and had warmed to the idea of a college education. Nelle Reagan put in a call to her Ronald, urging him to help. So, younger brother — who must have felt conflicted about lending his wiseass sibling a hand — sits down with Coach McKinzie, extols Moon's talents as a pass catcher at Dixon High, and wrangles him a spot on the football team along with a room at his TKE fraternity house. Entering Eureka as a freshman, Moon, though two and a half years older, is one year behind his kid brother. Moon wastes little time making an impression on the football field. "He made one of the most sensational runs of the season at Carthage, saving the game in the last few minutes of play," gushes the yearbook, according him the kind of adulation the younger Reagan could only long for. Dutch could hardly complain about being upstaged — in fact, since he did some of the sports reporting for the *Dixonian,* he may have written that glowing review — but years later Moon recalled his kid brother taking occasional advantage of his unaccustomed upperclassman status to wield the fraternity paddle against his elder with unrestrained vigor.

Dutch continued to fill out, putting 175 lean pounds on his willowy frame. By 1931, his senior season at Eureka, in a grainy, posed shot of him assuming a lineman's stance, he looks like he could do some damage. When I was very little, Dad and I would play pretend football on the living room rug. After allowing me to crash into him for a while, Dad would invariably take the opportunity to demonstrate, softly and in slow motion, how he could subdue much bigger opponents — "I once lined up against George Musso, who ended up playing for the Chicago Bears; he weighed nearly 300 pounds!" — by stunning them with an openhanded blow to the side of their head. I chose to take it on faith that the rules of football, in his day anyway, permitted such a practice. Looking at the photo of him crouched in his Eureka varsity uniform, poised to strike, my eyes are always drawn to the bandage wrapped around his loosely clenched left fist.

(For the record, Musso played college ball at Millikin University, weighing 255 pounds, before going on to become one of the largest of Chicago's Monsters of the Midway, at

270. In 1929, the year Reagan squared off against Musso, Millikin beat Eureka 45–6. Dutch also played against another giant and future NFL star, "Titan Tony" Blazine of Wesleyan.)

On a warm May afternoon I stroll with the college's current president, Dr. J. David Arnold, between Eureka's redbrick halls toward McKinzie Field. I have spent a pleasant day touring the campus, visiting the museum it devoted to my father, and posing for photos at the Peace Garden in front of a bronze bust of Dad that, inevitably, looks nothing like him. This version strikes a nice balance between a rabid leprechaun and James Brolin as conceived by a chain-saw artist.

The field itself — already named, during Dad's years at college, for his beloved coach — has changed little. "You'll notice there's no crown to it," my host points out. "Gets a little muddy when it rains. And if you're heading toward that goalpost," he gestures toward the far end, "you're actually traveling downhill."

So this unprepossessing sod is the patch of earth where, on autumn afternoons, Dutch Reagan would endeavor to join the pantheon of sporting gods. Naturally, there have been alterations to the scene over the intervening years. A press box has been installed along with more substantial bleachers than were called for during my father's day. Beyond the chain-link fence surrounding the gridiron, where once spread nothing but farm fields, housing tracts have begun to encroach. "And, of course, the field house is new," David tells me, referring to a self-consciously modern structure behind us. "In the old days, players would dress in their dorm rooms or fraternity houses, then walk to the game in uniform."

What I wouldn't give to travel back in time and take in that parade. I'll bet those walks were the highlight of my father's week — at least, once he became a starter. As a freshman scrub forced to wear his practice jersey, he may have experienced them as a humiliating gauntlet. But by the halfway point of that breakthrough sophomore season, he'd become an honored member of the tribe. Armored for combat in his maroon-and-gold uniform, on his way to storming the home field, he would stride through an effervescent bath of adulation — friends and classmates lining the paths to cheer on their gladiators: "Go get 'em, Dutch!" Dad's step, his cleats clattering on the walkways as he passed beneath the boughs of Eureka's sacred elms, would be springy with manly purpose. They were the select few, he and his teammates, fearless warriors defending the school's honor. After a couple of hours spent bashing, pummeling, and chasing across hallowed ground, the whole promenade would be repeated in reverse. In victory, the return walk would be accompanied by huzzahs and the admiring glances of campus belles; in tragic yet noble defeat, there would be consoling words to salve the heartaches of Eureka's bravest, and even more promisingly sympathetic looks from young women. This cavalcade of heroes lent itself beautifully to Dad's internal story; it must have felt like coming home — certainly more than did time spent in a stuffy classroom.

A word about my father's college academic record: He frequently joked that his real major was "extracurricular activities," his primary academic concern remaining eligible for the football squad. Standing in the archives of Eureka's library, I can see he wasn't kidding.

Dad had been an A student throughout grade school. Bernard J. Frazier, his English and drama teacher at Dixon High, found him "refreshing" but acknowledged he did B-level work there despite A-level ability. At Eureka — at least until his senior year — he appears to have slacked off considerably. His grades were mostly Cs. Elementary French, in which he received coaching from Mugs, seems to have been his strongest class — he pulled Bs. Sophomore year, despite his love for reading, he got Ds in American Literature and the English Romantic Movement. In the museum, director Dr. Brian Sjalko steers me to a paper on Wordsworth turned in by my father. Written in pencil, with cross outs and edits left in, it looks like a first draft hurriedly scribbled on the way to a pep rally — not an unimaginable scenario, come to think of it. The trend continued junior year, when Dutch managed a B in principles of sociology and a B– in a composition class. The rest of his grades were Ds and Cs — including a D in life of Christ. Things picked up during his senior year, though, with Bs in a series of economics classes. It seems almost sadistic to point out that one of his few Cs that final year came in a course called Reflective Living.

I certainly don't hold Dad's mediocre grades against him, nor do I think his C in U.S. history, for instance, had any bearing on his conduct in the Oval Office. I simply would have appreciated it if he'd been a bit more understanding — not to mention self-aware — when dealing with my own academic foibles.

In the winter of my freshman year in high school I received a letter from Dad. This was rarely a welcome development. My father was a faithful correspondent with old friends and supporters — provided they initiated contact — but missives addressed to his children were few and usually concerned some perceived failing on our parts. This letter would be no exception. After assuring me he didn't want to follow the example of some fathers who "wind up trying to relive their own youth by stage-directing their son's life," he warned that neither would he "cop out" by playing my "pal." Having set me up with his own version of good cop/bad cop, he cut to the chase:

You did fine in Ancient history — B-plus. You also had a B-plus in English 1, but an unsatisfactory effort. This makes the B-plus less to be desired than a lower grade if the lower grade represented the absolute best effort of which you were capable. But then comes a lesser grade, a C– in French 1, with a notation that, "The quality of work has diminished quite a bit." Again I say the C– would be all right with me if it represented your best try. This would be true also of the D in Algebra 1, but the effort was rated unsatisfactory and the teacher's notation read, "Ron has been relying on last year too long — he'd better force himself to get to work or he'll be in real trouble."

Tell you what: I'll trade you my D in algebra for your D in American lit. Or did your D represent your "absolute best effort"? I'm just saying a little perspective might have been in order.

Dad went on to warn that my "inner man" was in grave danger of devolving into a no-account pooter (my words, not his). My mother and he were "worried as to whether we've made that inner man as strong as he'll need to be sometime later in life when you call on him for help." This was one heaping plateful of foreboding over a couple of lousy grades. Could we not have discussed the matter in more reasonable tones on an upcoming weekend at home? Could he not have admitted, while we were on the subject, that he too had occasionally let his inner man stray from the academic straight and narrow?

After taking the opportunity to compare me unfavorably to a young California police officer who had lost a leg in a hit-and-run but would soon return to active duty nevertheless — my father having encouraged the highway patrol to set aside its long-standing regulations — Dad closed even more ominously: "Keep your eye on the price tag; some things are very expensive, and you pay for the rest of your life."

The problem here is not the sentiment. What responsible parent doesn't encourage his child to give his best effort? But Dad isn't really addressing me. He's writing to a character — the wayward son whose father (played by 1976 West Coast Father of the Year Ronald Reagan) must kindly, but sternly, set him straight. I'm getting the same treatment that his father, Jack, and more than a few potential drowning victims received: I've become a useful (if aggravating) symbol, a stock character providing contrast to his own, more Apollonian, example. The richer, ironic context surrounding us — namely, that we both did poorly in particular subjects in school — is ignored. Being reduced to a type, though, turns out to be a disquieting and not particularly inspiring experience. It certainly doesn't make you eager to crack a math book.

Back at Eureka, dogged persistence (on the gridiron, not the classroom) had paid off, if not in actual football stardom, at least in the opportunity to win a treasured varsity letter.

Dad's temper had almost cost him a shot at a college education; the flexibility of his own inner man, the portion of him he kept so private, had renewed that opportunity; but it was his sheer stubbornness and grit that, in the end, won over his football coach.

Have I mentioned he could be stubborn?

Sometime in the late 1970s — I had not yet left Los Angeles for a New York dance scholarship; Dad hadn't begun his run for the White House against Jimmy Carter — I drove north from Los Angeles to visit my folks at the 688-acre spread of oak, scrub, and rolling pasture atop the crest of the Santa Ynez Mountains they had recently acquired. Dad was what you'd call a gentleman rancher — raising just enough cattle to claim a tax deduction and keeping horses for the pleasure of riding them. But he had a do-it-yourself streak, preferring to handle most tasks, even heavy ones that would seem to call for a full work crew, by himself. When an especially large project was on order — say, digging a pond or putting up a fence fashioned from telephone poles — he would call on the help of a few longtime sidekicks who didn't mind getting dirty: Barney Barnett; former staff member Dennis LeBlanc; and, occasionally, me.

This particular day, Dad had determined,

provided us a perfect opportunity to make headway on the patio he had in mind for the area outside the front door of my parents' small ranch house. Because he wasn't one to take the easy route, we would not be doing anything as banal and unimaginative as pouring cement. Dad wanted to present his wife — bless his heart — with a patio fashioned of native sandstone gathered right there on the property.

We hitched up a trailer to the back of our old Jeep and set off for a spot he assured me had just the stones we were looking for, having scouted it out on horseback during a previous visit. Sure enough, there it was — a formidable tumble of pinkish-yellow rock panels in various shapes and sizes, most weighing upward of 100 pounds, some easily twice that.

Grunting and sweating, trying not to crush our fingers, we began humping the stones Dad judged patio-worthy into the little trailer. When its tires appeared ready to burst from the weight, Dad figured we had a full load, and back into the Jeep we piled. I assumed we would return to the house along the same route we had come. It was a bit circuitous but had the advantage of being mostly flat — not a bad thing when you're hauling a ton of rocks. Our only alternative was a shorter route that began with an un-invitingly steep climb along a narrow ridge.

Can you guess which route my father decided to take?

To our left the road fell away into a ragged slope of boulders similar to those we were pulling; on the opposite, passenger side, a couple of thousand brushy, plummeting, never gonna survive this feet below, was the Danish-themed tourist town of Solvang. Dad stomped on the clutch, shifted into first gear and started up the rutted, sloping fire road. It was grindingly slow going at first, but then, about two thirds of the way to the top, we stopped altogether. Dad's jaw was set, his foot pressed to the metal. The Jeep's engine strained, and it was becoming inescapably clear that the rocks were winning this battle. The laws of physics would not be denied. Slowly at first, but inexorably, we began to roll backward down the ridge, our trailer full of rocks leading the way.

It is questionable whether our Jeep was actually cut out to haul such a load in the first place. It certainly wasn't designed to be pulled ass-backward down a mountain by a runaway trailer overloaded with the makings of our new patio. As we began to pick up speed, bucking and jolting as the rocks asserted ever more control, I shot a worried glance at my father. Twisted around in his seat to face our new downhill direction, one hand on the wheel, the other arm casually draped over his seat back, he looked almost psychotically unconcerned. I was fighting to maintain sphincter control. As the Jeep began a sickening reverse fishtail, I considered abandoning ship. It was not so different from dismounting off the back of my old horse, Popeye, really. Sure, I'd have to take the Solvang route and, what with the trees, rocks, and rattlesnakes, would likely get pretty banged up, but staying with the Jeep was looking riskier by the nanosecond. When I looked back at Dad it was clear that, like the captain of the *Titanic,* he had no intention of going anywhere. Feeling a bit like the viola player in the ship's orchestra, launching into "Nearer My God to Thee" as icy brine rose about my ankles, I gritted my teeth and hung on.

Somehow Dad managed to maneuver the Jeep back onto level ground and brought us to a skidding halt. We both sat staring straight ahead for a moment, panting, breathless from our close call. Marinating in a sudden, soothing rush of endorphins, I naturally assumed my father would come to embrace sanity and take the safer road back to the house. "Oh, no. No need. We can make it," said Dad, as he began lining us up for another run at the ridge. I suppose that would have been the sensible time to hop out and start walking. But I could see we were now in this together.

Four tries it took: four lip-chewing, throttle-grinding, pant-sharting attempts before we finally conquered the ridge. By the third go — one in which we came heartbreakingly close to surmounting the crest before being yanked back once again toward oblivion — I could see it had become personal for Dad. To hell with the laws of physics! We were not about to be deterred by something as insubstantial as gravity.

In the end he triumphed — though the Jeep's transmission was never quite the same. The two of us jounced happily homeward with our trailer-load of rocks. To this day, the stone patio gives the old house a handsome, rough-hewn look.

Stubbornness does have its limits. Try as he might — and there was never anyone more crazily dedicated — Dutch was never going to be a real football star. The game he loved would never bring him the recognition he craved. His true talents, sometimes obscured by his fanatical devotion to the gridiron, lay elsewhere. But Eureka College provided him, at the very least, a venue in which to test those talents. One gift, on display almost as soon as he arrived on campus, would ultimately carry him to heights he could hardly have dared imagine as a college freshman. Another would provide him with a measure of fame and a good living for much of his adult life.

The larger world, once a source of anxiety for Dutch, had begun to beckon. Eureka, small and sheltering though it may be, will provide a stepping-stone to that world.

CHAPTER EIGHT
INTO THE WORLD

Standing with David Arnold, facing a wall of photographs of his predecessors as president of Eureka College, I search out one face in particular: Bert Wilson's.

"I kinda feel sorry for old Bert," says David with a slight shrug. "He was basically just trying to do what he was hired to do: cut the budget."

When Dutch Reagan first stepped onto the Eureka campus in September 1928, he found himself in the midst of a dispute already heatedly under way, and one about which he had little direct knowledge. He managed to attract some attention to himself with respect to it, nonetheless.

Eureka's enrollment had been dropping for years, and by my father's freshman year the situation had long since become critical. Revenue was lacking; endowments were inadequate. Wilson's plan, presented to the school's board of trustees on homecoming weekend that year, involved cutting the curriculum, combining subjects like math and physics, and, inevitably, letting go a few faculty members. On November 16, the board agreed to reduce Eureka's 15 departments to 8.

Teachers and students rebelled. A petition with 143 signatures — among them Ronald "Dutch" Reagan's — calling for Bert Wilson's resignation was presented to the board.

In response Wilson wrote, "The problem is a far greater one than the question of whether I am to continue as president. . . . The real question is, 'Can Eureka survive at all in face of the present trend in education and civilization?'"

In 1928 that was very much an open question. Eureka was competing for students and funding with more than two dozen other private colleges in Illinois as well as with the state university. The Disciples of Christ, as Wilson noted, "while giving it moral support, have never given in a large way to Eureka's endowment." He and the college were in a tough spot.

Wilson offered his resignation. The board refused. On the evening of November 27, just as students would normally be leaving for Thanksgiving break, board members ratified his plan. A few hours later, in the small hours of November 28, the campus bell began to toll, a prearranged signal summoning students and faculty — most wearing pajamas under overcoats — to an emergency meeting in the chapel. There they would decide whether to call a student strike in protest of the board's decision and once again demand Wilson's ouster.

Standing in front of a pipe organ on the small stage from which speakers addressed the decidedly prostrike, anti-Wilson crowd that chilly night, I stare out at the tall windows, high ceiling, and wooden floor and clap my hands. The sound comes bouncing back to me loud and harsh. I imagine the room filled with a couple of hundred boisterous students. It would have been pandemonium.

No one ever remembered what my father said from that stage that night — even his own much later recollection sounds like supposition. A considerable number of students took the opportunity to speak; Dutch may have been among the last. While Dad never remembered his exact words, he was much clearer about the audience's response:

For the first time in my life, I felt my words reach out and grab an audience, and it was exhilarating. When I'd say something,

they'd roar after every sentence, sometimes every word, and after a while, it was
as if the audience and I were one. When I
called for a vote on the strike, everybody
rose to their feet with a thunderous clap-
ping of hands and approved the proposal
for a strike by acclamation.

Whether my father was the one who called
for the vote that night is, truth be told,
unknown. That the motion to strike was
approved by acclamation is certain; that it
would be was a foregone conclusion going
in. My father certainly didn't have to win
over a crowd; they were already with him.
I'm sure virtually every other speaker —
provided they were sufficiently caustic about
President Wilson — received a similar response.

The fact that Dutch, as a freshman, was
speaking at all, though, is worthy of some
note. A young man named Les Pierce was
among the strike's ringleaders. He was also
head of Dutch's TKE fraternity house, which
had become the striker's de facto headquar-
ters. Whoever got the idea to include fresh-
men in the protest, it was probably Pierce
who nominated Dutch as an obvious choice
to speak for the incoming class. Like Coach
Mac, he may have found the new boy a bit

cocky and brash, but he seems to have recognized as well Dutch's verbal fluency and fearlessness before an audience.

As for my father, however sincerely he may have been committed to the academic issues involved, what really embedded the event in his memory was his connection to the crowd. He had spoken before staid church groups at his mother's instigation and performed in a number of school plays. He had already developed the routine of entertaining his buddies with reenactments of sporting events — theirs and others — delivered sports announcer–style into a broomstick masquerading as a microphone. He was not shy in front of a crowd. But this was evidently the first time he had ever felt the electric jolt of a rapturous audience response directed not at a fictional character mouthing someone else's words, but at Dutch Reagan himself, speaking his own words. That the experience, if not the text, of his brief speech — "as exciting as any I ever gave" — should remain lodged so prominently in his memory decades later is testament to the deep satisfaction he felt in front of that audience. He remembers the event like you'd remember your first sexual encounter: The details may be fuzzy, but the where has this been all my life feeling is abundantly clear.

His timing wasn't bad, either.

In the summer of 1976 I sat with my family and a gathering of friends and campaign staff in a high-roller box at the Kansas City Kemper Arena and watched as President Gerald Ford, having just narrowly defeated my father for the Republican presidential nomination, tried to wave him down to the stage for a public endorsement and unity photo op. Word had been relayed by the Ford camp: The president would like Governor Reagan to join him in front of the convention crowd. With the faces of everyone in that crowd now turned toward our box, I watched Dad's face.

His run against Ford, a sitting president of his own party, had not endeared him to everyone in the Republican establishment. Insurrectionary campaigns are not the usual GOP fare. Then, too, Ford was a severely compromised candidate, having never been elected to the presidency, having been appointed vice president instead by the disgraced Richard Nixon, who eventually resigned rather than face impeachment. The last thing he needed was a bruising nomination fight. But that's exactly what my father gave him, right down to the party's summer convention. Until a procedural vote the night before Ford's ultimate triumph,

281

the nomination remained nail-bitingly up in the air. The '76 Republican get-together was probably the last instance when any real drama occurred at one of these conventions.

Until that point my father had never lost a political race. While far from your stereotypical, aggressively competitive male, Dad didn't like to lose. I could tell he was disappointed. There had been talk of Ford's picking Dad as his vice presidential running mate for the fall election against the relatively unknown Georgia governor, Jimmy Carter. "Only the lead dog gets a fresh view," Dad told his advisers. He knew instinctively that second banana was not his natural role.

Ford, who desperately needed my father's imprimatur, was now waving energetically from the stage below. Dad may have wanted him to twist in the wind a little. "It's his night," I remember him saying. "Let him have it." He didn't budge. The minutes ticked past. Ford kept waving. The crowd — nearly half of which, after all, were Reagan supporters — began to cheer for Dad to take the podium. Still he bided his time. Chants of "Viva! Olé!" rose from the throng. He stood with my mother at the Plexiglas barrier at the front of our box and motioned for the crowd to sit, putting a finger to his lips to shush them. Their clamor for him to speak only increased.

My father hated to be rushed, and he never liked to perform when off balance. In an oral history recorded in 2002, Mike Deaver recalls that an arrangement between the Ford and Reagan camps had been reached whereby my father would only appear at the podium with Ford if the president himself publicly called for him — precisely what Ford was now doing. But because nobody on the Reagan team had thought Ford would actually go that far, Dad hadn't planned to speak that night, and so hadn't prepared any remarks. He wasn't about to appear in front of a large crowd without something meaningful to say. But the pressure — from the crowd and from the president, still motioning from the stage — was becoming acute. Sitting there, I wondered how long Dad could continue blowing Ford off. At a certain point his refusal to join the president would no longer look like modesty; it would amount to a pointed, public, nationally televised snub.

What was Dad up to? His reluctance was, in part, modesty. He had lost; it wasn't his night. And then there was the matter of ego. He had lost, and the "clean hatred" he once described feeling for opponents on the football field hadn't quite abated. He wasn't feeling particularly charitable toward Mr. Ford. But mostly, I think, he was figuring out what to say. Once he came up with words he felt were worthy of the occasion — words, moreover, that would leave little doubt in the minds of the assembled delegates that they had mistakenly nominated the inferior candidate — then and only then would he be willing to take the stage.

Ultimately, he had no choice. Down to the arena floor he went, to the stage, where he congratulated Ford, and finally to the microphone. In an interview years later with PBS, my mother recalled that, as they rushed downstairs that evening, Dad told her, "I haven't the foggiest idea what I'm going to say." I'm not sure that's true, but if it was, he came up with something pretty quickly. After discarding a few alternatives, I'm sure, Dad settled on a story he'd recently auditioned for family members. In remarks lasting no more than three or four minutes, he shared his thoughts about a time capsule recently buried in California, to be opened in 100 years. The people opening that capsule, he told the quieting crowd, would know whether the current generation had staved off nuclear annihilation. "They will know whether we met our challenge."

As soon as I heard him mention the time

capsule, I knew just where he was going. That did little to lessen the impact of his words in this particular setting. One might have expected a defeated politician under these circumstances to slap on a rictus grin and compliment the victor, issue a clarion call for party unity, and maybe give the opposition a good rogering. When was the last time you heard a runner-up — and a Republican, no less — use his moment in the consolation limelight to stump for nuclear disarmament? That night Dad sounded to me like a man on a mission, like a man who wanted to save the world. To the assembled delegates, he sounded like the guy they should have nominated. As their faces, many tear streaked and sobbing, played across the television monitor in our booth, it began to seem as if Dad had somehow won the night after all.

Dad finished up, gave his trademark plucky wave to the rapturously responding crowd, shook Ford's hand, and left him standing there like nobody's idea of a cool date to the prom.

Ford, of course, went on to lose to Jimmy Carter, as my father might well have had he managed to win the Republican nomination in '76. Ultimately, he won by losing.

Four years later, at another Republican

convention, this time in Detroit, my father and Ford would meet again. Dad had already secured the nomination, but the choice of a vice president remained open. Some people were pushing for the former president. Ford, who might have been itching for a rematch with Carter, seemed to envision a sort of co-presidency, with him taking the lead on foreign affairs — an arrangement that wouldn't have appealed to my father any more than being Ford's VP had four years earlier. While Mike Deaver and I crouched in the hallway outside the door of a hotel suite, trying vainly to catch snippets of their conversation, Dad and Ford discussed the matter. I remember thinking that if Dad were to pick Ford, acceding to the former president's demand for a virtually coequal role in the White House, it would contradict something vital about him of which I felt quite certain. In the end, he went with George H. W. Bush.

Did my father's experience speaking before a hall full of pumped-up student strikers at Eureka somehow lead to his appearance in a Kansas City convention hall nearly a half century later? That would be a difficult conclusion to draw based on the facts. The circumstances and content of his college remarks were relatively unimportant. He didn't think of himself, at the time, as being involved in anything like a political movement; his mind was as far from a smoke-filled room as it's possible to get. It was all about him and the crowd. He could just as well have been enjoying accolades at a sporting event or acting performance, or while rescuing a kitten from a tree. Most meaningful was the intensity and focus of the audience response: howlingly appreciative and, for a brief instant, trained solely on him.

Not that Dutch was oblivious to politics. He had inherited from both parents an interest in current affairs and was involved in student government in both high school and college. But these activities were a means to an end: feeling connected to the world; being where the action was; and, as always, swinging attention his way. Taking up acting was a natural choice for someone of his temperament.

CORYDON: Oh, Thyrsis, now for the first time I see
This wall is actually a wall, a thing
Come up between us, shutting me away
From you . . . I do not know you any more!

THYRSIS: No, don't say that! . . . How did it start?

CORYDON: I do not know . . . I do not know . . . I think

I am afraid of you! — You are a stranger!

Dutch Reagan's assaying the role of Thyrsis for the Eureka Players in *Aria da Capo,* Edna St. Vincent Millay's poetic response to human folly, militaristic and otherwise — grotesquely played-out during the recent world war — provides biographers with a perfect segue into my father's much later détente with Mikhail Gorbachev. Thyrsis and Corydon, two actors portraying Greek shepherds in a play within the play, construct a wall dividing them. Too late they realize that the wall, however insubstantial, has meant the death of them both.

On April 11, 1930, the Eureka Players participated in the Fifth Annual Theater Tournament at Northwestern University. Mugs Cleaver was in the cast as an oblivious social butterfly, Columbine. Playing opposite Dutch as Corydon was his football teammate and quarterback, Bud Cole. The Players — Eureka didn't really have a drama department per se — were awarded third prize among nine groups competing. Dutch Reagan was named among the six best actors of the tournament. Perhaps more im-

288

portant, he was encouraged toward a goal he had been secretly nurturing for some time when the director of Northwestern's School of Speech, Garret Leverton, was impressed enough to advise him to pursue a career in acting.

Dutch had been an avid moviegoer since childhood. He and Moon had always hoarded their pennies for afternoon escapes to Dixon's theater. There they watched as silent film acquired a voice. Dutch was particularly swept away by westerns — not only by the image of a lone hero saving the day, but by the background vistas as well, with their unfamiliar, wide-open landscapes. Clean and uncluttered, these alien deserts and high plains allowed a man to see trouble coming from a long way off. They seemed a fitting arena for great deeds. Having performed the real thing often enough, he of course grasped that the flickering figures on the screen were only miming heroism. Still, there was more than one way to save the day. Dutch knew, too, that Hollywood actors earned shocking amounts of money disporting on camera. He had seen their photographs in glossy magazines, wheeling along palm-lined streets in elegant motorcars, the women beside them exuding sex. Such a lifestyle certainly had its appeal. But money available in what, to a Midwest boy in Depression-era America, seemed ludicrous amounts offered a more meaningful opportunity to play the hero. By 1930 the crash had brought down not only Wall Street, but Jack's Fashion Boot Shop as well. With family finances tight, Jack was now peddling shoes on the road; Nelle had gone back to work as a seamstress. Imagine if Dutch were somehow able to become one of those people he watched on the movie house screen. He could live a glamorous life and still have plenty of money left over to ensure the comfort and security of his family. That would be heroism of an entirely different order.

There was just one problem: The whole idea was lunacy. Who did he think he was? Tom Mix? Ramon Novarro? Douglas Fairbanks? Small-town boys from rural Illinois didn't just swan off to Hollywood and become big movie stars. And they didn't even talk up the possibility, if they knew what was good for them. Dutch might be something of a local hero for his lifeguarding exploits; he was reassuringly active in his mother's church, all the while chastely dating the pastor's daughter; and he was, granted, absurdly handsome — though in a boyish, wholesome sort of way. Looks notwithstanding, none of those qualities necessarily pointed to a career among the louche gypsies of the West Coast film community.

Dutch kept his thoughts of movie stardom mostly to himself, confiding just enough in Mugs to earn her disapproval. While he kept his public persona wrapped up in football, college boosterism, student government, and lifeguarding, the private Dutch was entertaining larger dreams. The rural towns of his youth, once so comforting in their closeness, had begun to seem confining. He was beginning to see a place for himself in the world beyond the Rock River and the familiar fields of his youth. But there were still lessons to be learned, even in Dixon.

Any discussion with my father concerning racial issues would inevitably evoke the same reminiscence about a road trip taken during his senior football season at Eureka. Searching for a place to spend the night while on their way home from a game, the team happens to stop in Dad's beloved hometown. Under the coach's rules, there's no question of letting my father spend a night under his parents' roof; the team sticks together. So Dad accompanies Mac to the front desk of a downtown hotel, where they discover that plenty of rooms are available for everyone but the two black players on the team. I'll let my father pick it up from there with the version presented in *An American Life:*

"Then, we'll go someplace else," Mac said.

"No hotel in Dixon is going to take colored boys," the manager shot back.

Mac bristled and said all of us would sleep on the bus that night. Then I suggested another solution: "Mac, why don't you tell those two fellows there isn't enough room in the hotel for everybody so we'll have to break up the team; then put me and them in a cab and send us to my house."

Mac gave me a funny look; he'd just had a chance to observe firsthand what the people of Dixon thought of blacks, and I'm sure he had his doubts my parents would think much of the idea. "You sure you want to do that?" he asked.

He was as sure as he could be. There would be no problem at the Reagan residence: Jack's views on race were well-known, and good-hearted Nelle, as my father wrote, "was absolutely color blind when it came to racial matters." Dad and his two black teammates arrive unannounced and are welcomed without so much as a sidelong glance. Dad gets to pay a visit home. Everyone sleeps in a warm bed. The hotel manager makes a few bucks. All good. Everyone's happy. End of story.

Or is it? First, Dad's two black teammates had to have been aware of exactly what was going on when they were dispatched to the Reagan home. (One of the men, Franklin "Burky" Burkhardt, who lined up at center next to my father, confirmed this in an interview years later.) It would be surprising if the whole team hadn't caught on to the situation pretty quickly, so there being any notion of sparing people's feelings seems questionable. Then there's the matter of rewarding racism. Mac's instinct was exactly right: I'm not going to put one dime in your bigoted pocket. It's not hard to imagine the coach's taking advantage of the incident to deliver a lesson to his team: "Now, boys, you know we stick together as a team; and sometimes that means we all have to sacrifice together on behalf of something much bigger than a game . . ." Instead, in my father's rendition, Dutch becomes the center of attention as, with nothing but good intentions, I'm sure, he attempts to ease his way (and others') around an unpleasant brush with the rawness of life. I can't help wondering if Dad shared the truth behind the unexpected sleepover with his father and, if he did, what Jack had to say about it.

That Jack was even home that particular night was something of an oddity. After a brief, unhappy stint working at the Dixon Home for the Feebleminded — where, a few years earlier, his elder brother, William, had died, finally succumbing to the ravages of his "alcoholic psychosis" — he had been living apart from the family, dividing his time between sales trips on the road and stints in a little dump of a shoe store in Springfield, Illinois, 140 miles to the south. My father remembers its "garish orange paper ads plastered over the windows" and its "one cheap iron bench" from a visit he and Moon paid while passing through town on yet another trip with the football team. This was not a contented moment for the family. Not only were they missing Moon's cement job paycheck, but the Fashion Boot Shop in Dixon, in which Jack had invested so much hope, was a memory. With the Depression in full swing, people were no longer in the mood to buy fancy footwear. Jack had been traveling, selling his wares on commission. Plying the back lanes, of course, offered opportunities to indulge his taste for whiskey and, perhaps, other transgressions. By the time he began spending time in Springfield, there were rumors of another woman, perhaps a professional, to whom Jack's meager dollars were being siphoned before they could find their way home. Christmas Eve of that year brought more bad news: He received a blue slip notice in the mail — yet another job lost. "Well, it's a hell of a Christmas present," he said, eyes still riveted to what he had hoped would be a bonus check.

Jack, too, had had a run-in with bigotry around this time and showed himself to be cut more in the Coach Mac mold, less a conciliator than young Dutch. While out peddling shoes he stopped one evening at a hotel whose desk clerk told him, "You'll like it here, Mr. Reagan; we don't permit a Jew in the place." "I'm a Catholic," Jack replied, on his way out the door. "If it's come to the point where you won't take Jews, then some-day you won't take *me*, either." He slept the night in his car, contracting pneumonia, and soon thereafter had the first of the heart attacks that would eventually kill him.

There remains the question of his son's appreciation of the racial situation in his hometown. No hotel in Dixon is going to take colored boys? Could we be talking about another Dixon, one not so thoroughly rhapsodized by my father?

It was a small universe where I learned the standards and values that would guide me for the rest of my life. . . .

Almost everybody knew one another, and because they knew one another, they tended to care about each other. If a family down the street had a crisis — a death or a serious illness — a neighbor brought them dinner that night. If a farmer lost his barn to a fire, his friends would pitch in and help him rebuild it.

Who in this golden-toned little Dixon wouldn't have been aware that black people weren't welcome to spend the night?

Apparently, everyone but Dutch. Imagine him on the bus as the gang pulled in to town: regaling teammates with its sundry virtues; pointing out the sights — here the Rock River where he lifeguards all summer, there the playing fields of his high school glory days. He was proud of his river-straddling town, the one place he had stayed long enough to truly call home. The phrase "shining city on a hill" may yet have been unfamiliar to him on that distant evening, but I have little doubt he was already laying the foundations of that city in his mind, using Dixon as a prototype. With an air of proprietary familiarity, knowing just where they might stay, he would have guided the driver to the hotel. At age 21, could he not have foreseen how the hotel check-in would play out? No amount of nearsightedness could have made him blind to the prevailing racial attitudes in his hometown. As an avid moviegoer, he would have been familiar with the fact that the local theater was segregated — whites-only in the orchestra section, blacks relegated to the balcony. Moon, in typical Reagan fashion, had a best friend who was black; when they went to a movie together, Moon would join him in the cheap seats, which suggests that 1930s' Dixon was liberal enough that this transgression didn't provoke a lynching. While Dixon itself wasn't very different in its racial attitudes from other towns scattered across rural America during the Dust Bowl thirties, Dutch just didn't seem attuned to them.

My father must have been terribly embarrassed that night at the hotel. All that bragging on his hometown, and now his team would have to spend the night shivering on the bus? Better to come up with a face-saving way out that was, in any case, readily at hand. And the larger principle involved? That beloved Dixon utterly failed, in one important regard at least, to live up to the ideals espoused not only by Coach McKinzie but, even more explicitly, by Dutch's own parents? That was an unattractive reality that had to be wrapped in enough amber-tinted gauze that it became muffled and indistinct — a bad thing, as had to be acknowledged, but safely contained and marginalized.

My father will write, much later, about what he calls "tumors" of racism in America — a suitably ugly metaphor perhaps, but one suggesting that the nature of bigotry in this country is one of aberrant and isolated disease. The truth — that this brute manifestation of ignorance was, especially during the period of my father's youth, pervasive and systemic, not only in his hometown but in the greater "shining city" that was his dream of America — would always be too much for him to bear. Reciting the hotel story to me years later when I was growing up, he would invariably omit the detail that the town in question was, in fact, his own. I was always uneasy, even as a kid, with the racist hotel owner getting off the hook. As a young teenager hearing the anecdote repeated, I once questioned Dad about how it was that Jack and Nelle lived close enough that they could supply lodging for the night. He grew vague, allowing only that they lived "nearby."

The episode exposes Dad's need to excise ugliness from his view of life. It also presents him with an inevitable conundrum: If racism existed as tumors in his boyhood America, then his venerated hometown was a malignancy within the larger community; if, on the other hand, Dixon was fairly typical for the times in its bigotry, then the America of his youth — even the northerly parts — cannot represent anything approaching a "shining city" for all. These were the sorts of contradictions Dad was never able to resolve in his own mind, contradictions he instead edited his way around.

At the same time, the whole business serves to highlight the wonderful strangeness of the Reagan family in Dixon, and, presumably, other places they had lived. In a staunchly Republican county, they were active Democrats. Among tight-lipped farm folk, their theatrical forays must have made them seem like florid sensualists. A small town full of gossip could hardly have missed Jack's drinking jags, the couple's audible rows, and those suspicions of extramarital womanizing. They were decidedly not Old Dixonites, the Reagans. They were odd. They were different.

It's 1932. Herbert Hoover is still president but won't be for long if Jack and Nelle Reagan, who are avidly supporting Franklin Roosevelt, have anything to say about it. The Great Depression is well under way.

Thirteen million Americans are out of work. Both government and private companies are cutting wages by up to 30 percent and reducing work hours in a desperate effort to boost employment. In Washington, D.C., World War I vets march to demand early payment of their promised cash bonuses. Al Capone is convicted of tax evasion.

Overseas, Benito Mussolini heads Italy's government. Joseph Stalin is consolidating power in Russia, where some five million famine-stricken peasants are starving to death. Adolf Hitler is one year away from being elected Germany's chancellor. In London, the Hunger Marchers Army protests a lack of food, while, in India, Mahatma Gandhi begins a hunger strike to protest Britain's caste separation laws.

Charles Lindbergh's baby will be kidnapped and murdered. Amelia Earhart will become the first woman to fly solo across the Atlantic, six years after Lindbergh. This year Americans will, for the first time, begin paying a tax on gasoline.

In the 21 years since Dutch Reagan's birth, much of the world has changed drastically. In America, industrialization, a swelling movement of people from farms to cities, women's suffrage, and new modes of communication and entertainment have transformed landscapes both physical and mental. And, of course, the automobile has thoroughly altered everyone's sense of time, travel, and distance. Dutch no longer wakes to the stamping of horses hooves but to the revving of an engine and the smell of petroleum exhaust.

There will be one last summer on the Rock River, with a few more notches to be carved on Dutch's driftwood log. Soon, though, he will have to decide whether and how to find his place in the new reality being created beyond the boundaries of Dixon.

Who is this young man — now among the mere 7 percent of his generation to receive a college education — perched atop his lifeguard chair?

I take a last pass through his college memorabilia searching for stray clues. As far as anyone has been able to determine, only one of the Eureka yearbooks held by the Reagan Library — from his sophomore year — actually belonged to my father. Scanning it eagerly, I look for inscribed messages from friends. What hints to his early personality and youthful character might there be? Not many, as it turns out. A couple of football teammates and frat brothers have made a minimal effort — "Yours in the bond, Al" — and the freshman class vice president,

Marie Brodie, who may have simply been infatuated with the handsome young man a year ahead of her, hopes he continues with his acting. Then I come across this curious entry next to a picture of a woman in the senior class, Celestine McCarver: "To 'Rager', whom <u>they</u> call 'The Wooden Man' — but 'I like you that way!'" The note is signed "Susanne herself." Is Susanne actually Celestine? Was she a friend? A crush? Someone who shared a drama class? Was the assumed name a private joke between them? No telling. But more intriguing is the allusion to The Wooden Man. Who were <u>they</u> — seniors? classmates? — and why did they refer to my father that way?

In its definition of "wooden" *Webster's* dictionary offers "lacking ease or flexibility" and "awkwardly stiff." Did Dad's classmates consider him a prig? Had his gung-ho Dixon spirit — which, naturally, had morphed into a Eureka spirit — become tiresomely earnest? Was his single-minded fixation with football so tedious it tested even the patience of his jock fraternity brothers?

Perhaps his children weren't the first to believe that Dad was a bit of a square.

By college graduation, a rather successful square, we must acknowledge: football letterman; award-winning thespian; Eureka's best swimmer; president of the student council; more or less officially engaged to an A-list girl. Voluble and gregarious, he has become one of the campus's best organizers. During his senior year he has finally managed to raise his grades into respectable territory. His face and body have continued to mature gracefully. At six feet one and a half inches, with wavy center-parted hair and his trademark lopsided grin, he is good-looking enough even with his glasses to be an obvious standout in photographs with his fellows. There is a general assumption that he is going places, though by places most of his classmates are probably thinking no farther than Des Moines, or maybe Chicago. People have their own ideas about where Dutch belongs. Pastor Ben Cleaver, his fiancée's father, has noticed his facility with words, how naturally he seems to connect with an audience. It would please the formidable clergyman if his daughter were to marry a young man destined for the pulpit. It would suit Mugs as well. Jack, meanwhile, was likely advising a more practical approach. Montgomery Ward was looking for a salesman in its sporting goods department. With his athletic background and local lifeguarding notoriety, Dutch would be a perfect fit. Only Nelle might have been dreaming as big as her son. She'd always had him pegged for big things, had always thought him "perfectly wonderful."

And Dutch? What images of the future illuminate his own mind in that final season on the Grand Detour?

Standing with my back to a formidable oak just across a stretch of lawn from where Lowell Park's old pier and waterslide used to stand, I gaze out at the Rock River running brown and turbid in the afternoon light and try to put myself, if you will, in my father's singlet.

From his chair beneath his favorite tree, Dutch Reagan will bring to bear on his future endeavors a formidable set of talents. His physical beauty is a benefit he has long since recognized. Combined with his verbal fluency, it lends him a charisma that makes people want to do things for him. He lacks the patience for extended intellectual rigor but possesses nonetheless a keen instinctive intelligence and, as ever, an intensely active imagination. He feels himself to be an agent of destiny, though what that destiny might be he doesn't yet know. Somehow, though, he is certain his worth will be recognized. Like other young men that Depression summer, he faces an inhospitable labor environment, but he has great confidence in himself, even

304

a kind of brashness. He bets his friends that he will be earning the princely sum of $5,000 per week — an absurd amount of money for someone from Dutch's background — within five years. This is an unusually open admission of ambition on Dutch's part — a bit of the eager inner Reagan rising to the surface. In future years he will become more thoroughly adept at masking his personal drive. In public he will appear unfailingly modest though, inside, he thrills to receive acclaim. In private he will so eschew any hint of personal desire as to be incapable of acknowledging his craving for even a second helping of my wife's irresistible apple pie. Believe me, he really did want more pie (and got it, of course).

Like Jack, who lifted his sights from the floor of a grain elevator to the proprietorship of a fashionable boutique — and like Nelle, for that matter, who, had she been born 20 years later in a big city, might well have chosen a career in the theater over devotion to church — Dutch harbors an unquenchable flame of ambition. He believes in his dreams. He may apply for that Monty Ward job as a fallback, but his sights are secretly — and to Mugs's profound dismay — set on Hollywood. He will try radio first, as a stepping-stone, make some ready cash, buy himself a shiny Nash convertible, then head for the West Coast. He is young. The sap is rising. He has no real idea yet how indifferent to the desires of a handsome, well-meaning heroic type the world can be. Time, he feels, is on his side.

Just shy of five years on, he will surprise everyone — except, perhaps, himself — by winning his wager.

In the years ahead, he will find more fame than even his imaginative young mind could have dared conjure. He will continue to surprise his friends from the old days as he makes his way through careers in radio, movies, and television. With his first taste of Hollywood success, he will move his parents out to the coast, into the first home to which they've ever held a deed, salving Jack's pride by offering him a "job" sorting his fan mail. He will never become quite the movie star that he hoped to be. His once promising career will be sidetracked by World War II and never really recover. Having flirted with communism, he will later, as president of the Screen Actors Guild, become a staunch anticommunist. During an intensely painful period in the late forties, his first marriage to Jane Wyman will dissolve; then while his ex awaits an Oscar for her role in *Johnny Belinda,* he'll endure a freezing winter shoot in foggy postwar London, only to watch helplessly — but good-naturedly — as newcomer Richard Todd steals *The Hasty Heart* from both him and Patricia Neal. In 1949, adding physical insult to emotional injury, he will shatter his femur sliding into first base while playing in a charity softball game, leaving him on crutches and holed up at his mother's house. Skies will begin to lift, though, late in the year, when he meets an actress from Chicago 10 years his junior. Nancy Davis will become, for the duration, the most important person in his life, the only one ever to match Nelle's fervent devotion. Finally, entering politics, he will travel further and achieve more than anyone who watched him pull swimmers from the river in those early Depression years could have predicted.

But those are stories for another time. We are concerned here primarily with the formative years of his story's beginning. Every tale needs an ending, however, so we will leapfrog far ahead now — with some observations from his later years — to the very end.

As we leave Rock River, though, let's take one last look back over our shoulders at the watchful young man on his chair, his eyes fixed on the river's danger spots. He still has plenty of growing to do and many parts yet to play. But his mold has been cast. For the entirety of his long life, he will remain, at heart, dedicated to the one role that came entirely naturally to him: lifeguard.

More than a half century hence, even as the powers he now feels burgeoning within have begun to wane, Dutch Reagan will try to save the world.

CHAPTER NINE
HOME AND FREE

On June 5, 2004, moments before 1:00
P.M., my father opened his eyes for the last
time. Gathered around his bed, which he
had scarcely left for months, were his wife,
Nancy, daughter Patti, and me, along with
a nurse and physician. His decline had
proceeded through a series of plateaus and
precipices for more than a decade, drawing
him steadily further from us. All along, even
as his mind was collapsing, Dad's doctors
had marveled at the soundness of his body:
His hair remained full and soft, still need-
ing a trim every couple of weeks; his heart
and lungs continued to function like those
of a much younger man. His face, too, free
of care as he lay, day after day, in restful
somnolence, had lost many of its worry lines
and wrinkles. Strangely, as time passed, he
began to look younger. Disease and death,
though, would have the final word. Hearing
from my mother that he had stopped eating

and taking in fluids, and that his kidneys had begun to fail, my wife and I returned early that June from our yearly vacation. It was clear to all of us that the close of a long and remarkable life was imminent. It was a surprise, though, after so long, to see his eyes again, burning and bluer than I remembered.

In the days following Dad's death, we traveled back and forth across the country with his body aboard Air Force One (graciously provided by President George W. Bush), enacting the various rituals of passage accorded a deceased head of state. Arriving in Washington, D.C., we were greeted by what seemed to be the entire population of the city lining the broad avenues along which we carried my father toward Capitol Hill. We had known, of course, that Dad's funeral and his various memorial services would be widely covered media events, but we were stunned by the outpouring of emotion and the magnitude of the public's response.

Whatever else you might say about the Reagans, we are, by dint of circumstance, training, and perhaps genetics, troupers. We understood that, for the time being, we would be doing our grieving in public. We showed up on schedule. We entered and exited on cue. We hit our marks. Our lines were blessedly few but uttered with grace and conviction. Mostly we stood by in dignified silence, which, as it happens, afforded plenty of time for reflection.

Beneath the soaring dome of the capitol, my father, in his flag-draped coffin, was set to rest by a military honor guard atop the catafalque that had once borne the body of Abraham Lincoln. There could be no more pointed reminder that we had come very close to enacting these very solemnities decades earlier.

On March 30, 1981, my wife and I were in Lincoln, Nebraska, where I was performing with the Joffrey Ballet's training company. We were having lunch in a hotel dining room when the agent in charge of my Secret Service detail approached our table with a look on his face that suggested he would not be the bearer of glad tidings. "We've gotten word that someone has fired some shots at your father," he whispered, leaning in close so as not to broadcast the news to the entire restaurant. "They don't think he was hit."

Back in our room a couple of minutes later, we spoke with a member of my mother's staff, who was less encouraging. "He was hit, but we don't think it's too bad."

When I was very young, probably no more

than three or four, I delighted in watching my father on television. At that age I imagined that he was talking directly to me and that I, in turn, could talk back to him. Babbling away, I would become cross when he didn't seem to be paying attention. My mother would calm me by explaining that he was too busy at the moment doing his job, but would certainly want to hear what I had to say when he got home. On one occasion during these tender years — it may have been an airing of his final film, *The Killers,* or perhaps the 1955 western, *Tennessee's Partner* — I had the misfortune of seeing his character get shot. I was disconsolate, requiring an extensive review of acting versus reality to bring me out of my funk. As it turned out, seeing your father shot for real is a lot worse.

Video of the shooting was being played over and over on every channel: Dad emerges from a door of the Washington Hilton Hotel, angling across the sidewalk bordering T Street and heading for the presidential limousine with his usual bouncy step, happily waving to a few well-wishers off to his right across the street. As he turns back to his left, right arm still aloft and waving, a popping erupts off camera, and mundane news file wallpaper becomes, for the next couple of minutes, chaotic war zone footage.

A look of concern crosses my father's face just as detail leader Jerry Parr grabs him from behind and shoves him into the backseat of the limo. Agent Tim McCarthy, meanwhile, who had been standing just to my father's left, pirouettes backward with a bullet in his abdomen. I recognize Mike Deaver's face ducking low past the camera as he dives for cover. White House press secretary Jim Brady and a D.C. police officer, Tom Delahanty, are facedown in expanding pools of blood. A bullet has struck Brady in the head; Delahanty has been hit in the neck. Buried in a scrum of cops and agents, now relieved of the cheap .22 caliber pistol he'd picked up in a Dallas pawnshop, is a young man with a personality disorder and delusions of grandeur. When we make his acquaintance, John Hinckley's resemblance to John Lennon's recent killer, Mark David Chapman — doughy, beady-eyed, features too small for his face — will be striking.

Arriving back in the capital aboard a Lear jet rented by the Secret Service (direct service between Lincoln and Washington, D.C., is uncommon, and no one was in the mood for dealing with a connecting flight), my wife and I headed straight for George Washington University Hospital. When we

313

reached the floor where my mother was waiting, Dad was still in surgery. Mike Deaver pulled me aside as soon as I arrived, saying, "Thank God you're here." I gathered immediately that the situation was extremely dire. My mother, unsurprisingly, looked pale and shaken. She seemed even tinier than usual, and more fragile, in a room full of bustling, officious bodies moving in and out, none of them telling her what she wanted to hear: Her husband was still alive, he would make it. Her prime directive for 30 years had been to support, nurture, and protect my father. Now, in his moment of greatest peril, with his life hanging by a thread, she was locked out of the room, helpless.

In the moments after the shooting, Mike had managed to get himself into a car following the presidential limo. Initially the motorcade had headed toward the White House, where the president would be safe from further attack. Inside the limo there was no immediate indication that Dad had been wounded. But within minutes he was complaining of chest pain and having trouble breathing, and then he began coughing up a pink froth — blood coming from his lungs. Still, Dad's assumption was that his rib had been broken and his lung punctured when Agent Parr dove on top of him as he shoved him into the car. In any case, Parr instantly ordered the car diverted to the hospital, a decision that, in all likelihood, saved Dad's life.

Ever the showman, my father would not drop out of character until he was safely out of view backstage. Watching him climb out of the car and give his pants their customary hitch, Mike later remembered thinking that his boss must be fine. He seemed utterly normal, his usual self. As soon as he crossed the threshold of the hospital doors, however, Dad staggered and dropped to one knee. A frantic race began to keep him alive.

Dad's blood pressure barely registered. He was obviously bleeding internally, but as yet no one had located the spot where the bullet had entered his body. Hinckley had loaded his pistol with a type of exploding bullet charmingly marketed as a Devastator. It was his sixth and final shot that first hit not Dad but the armor-plated side of the presidential limousine. The armor did its job admirably well, but with disastrous consequences. As it was deflected, the bullet flattened into a dime-sized disk before striking my father, slicing into his chest beneath his left arm and lodging in his left lung, barely an inch from his heart, still unexploded. His doctors ultimately — courageously — removed the slug, knowing it could detonate at any second.

Much has been made of my father's joking with doctors and nurses that day: "Honey, I forgot to duck." "All in all, I'd rather be in Philadelphia." And, to his surgeons, "Please tell me you're all Republicans." Del Wilber, a journalist working on a book focused exclusively on the assassination attempt, has shared with me the news that Dad actually tried out that last line earlier as emergency room personnel were frantically cutting his clothing from his body in an attempt to locate an entry wound. Understandably distracted, they were in no mood for humor and didn't provide the response he was looking for. So, thinking it was a pretty good line nonetheless, he filed it away for use at a more opportune moment — like being wheeled into surgery. There he got the properly appreciative reaction, as the lead surgeon, Dr. Joseph Giordano — in point of fact, a liberal Democrat — told him, "Today, Mr. President, we're all Republicans."

Bleeding to death with a bullet in his chest, and he's doing shtick. That was so Dad. This may sound bizarre — and indeed, it is — but anyone reading this who knew him will be nodding and thinking: *He was embarrassed to be putting everyone out*. As much as he loved to be fussed over, Dad hated being in a position of physical weakness and suffered excruciating discomfort whenever he was the cause of any upset. The idea that schedules had been disrupted, people's routines upended, that he, however unwittingly, had been an agent of chaos would have filled my stricken father with dismay. He was the one meant to bring order to the world. He was supposed to be the lifesaver.

Plus, no matter how calamitous the circumstances, he just couldn't help himself when presented with a fresh audience.

In October 1978, the foothills above Los Angeles performed their periodic trick of seeming to self-immolate. This is an event native Angelinos take in stride, like earthquakes rattling the dishes or celebrities getting themselves in trouble. In a 1961 version of the recurring conflagration, my family's Pacific Palisades home suffered a near miss: Our Malibu ranch lost its stables (the horses were rescued well ahead of time), and I had been evacuated from my preschool classroom just hours before it burned to the ground. Such is the price of living amid tinder-dry chaparral.

Now yet another major fire was threatening my childhood home. I got the call from my mother while working the reception desk at the ballet studio where I had a "scholarship"; i.e., I scrubbed floors and performed other tasks in exchange for a modest stipend and free classes. Mom was gathering up the family photos and preparing to throw the silverware into the swimming pool. The fire had by now reached Rustic Canyon, leaving only one brush-choked ridge separating my folks from an inferno. If the flames topped the crest, they would evacuate. I had ridden to work that day with my roommate, another aspiring dancer on scholarship. I grabbed him, along with his girlfriend, Doria — as it happens, the woman who would, a little more than two years later, do me the honor of becoming my wife — and we piled into his old VW bug and rattled off toward the mushroom cloud of smoke billowing over the Santa Monica Mountains.

Aside from that brief childhood trip to Saigon during the Vietnam War, I've never been in a war zone. I imagine, though, that it must be something like what the three of us encountered as we reached the firefighters' front lines. The smoke was chokingly thick, smelling of natural brush but laced also with the acrid scent of synthetic materials from the homes the blaze had already consumed. The noise and flashing lights from battalions of fire trucks, the helicopters circling over-

head, the brown pall blotting out the sun —
all added to the sense of End Times bedlam.

After convincing a fire marshal that my
parents were up ahead where the smoke was
glowing red, we were allowed to proceed
across fat pythons of fire hose with a warning to watch out for ourselves, and that we
were on our own.

Remember the scene in *The Wizard of Oz*
where the ostensibly Mighty Oz arrives in
a puff of green smoke? Magnify that by a
factor of one hundred, color it orange, and
sprinkle in a dash of *Apocalypse Now,* with
flame retardant–dumping choppers diving
among blooming fireballs, and you have
some idea what confronted us as we reached
my parents' dead-end street — the last street
before the flaming defile of Rustic Canyon.

The neighboring houses looked deserted.
No fire trucks were in evidence. As we
rounded the last curve before reaching my
folks' driveway, I looked up to see a lonely
light burning in the window of their den.

It strikes me as odd, looking back — maybe
it's a comment on the evanescent nature of
celebrity in America, or maybe another example of my father's solitary nature — that
a former film and television actor who had
recently been governor of the state, who had
nearly captured his party's nomination for

the presidency only two years earlier and was widely considered to be a front-runner for the next go-round, would be all alone with his wife, left to his own devices, as a major wildfire bore down on them. Thank goodness a couple of ballet dancers with their young lady friend in tow were on hand to help out.

Dad, dressed in one of the cotton jump-suits he favored for puttering around the house, let us in with a smile, then led the way to the den, where he had laid out some maps of the local terrain. These, I gathered, were left over from the fire years earlier. My mother bustled past, clutching photo albums and looking relieved to see what would have to pass for the cavalry. Her default mode being anxiety, she needed no prodding to appreciate the gravity of the situation. A slight shift in the wind, an ember carried aloft, and houses would start combusting all around us. Dad, as usual, seemed absurdly calm, as if breakneck escape before an advancing wall of flame wasn't something he'd planned on but might, when all was said and done, turn out to be kind of a kick — and fodder for a good story besides.

Having detailed the grim view from outside the parental bubble, I volunteered to take a walk up the fire road in back of the house to see how much time we had left — a truly absurd idea when you think about it. I followed a childhood path through the foliage at the border of the property, roommate at my heels, and stepped onto the dirt road winding upward toward the direction of the fire. I had first climbed this road as a four-year-old, following it with my father to a flat hilltop, where we would fly kites. I kept glancing above us, toward the top of the ridge, alert for any sign of brush igniting. Wheezing and hacking, eyes stinging, we stumbled through the smoke and heat to an overlook just in time to see the burning front of the fire, a roaring, shrieking maelstrom, passing by the end of our street and heading down canyon toward Sunset Boulevard. Nothing seemed to be coming over the ridge. My parents and their home had once again escaped. Looking down, I noticed the rubber soles of my tennis shoes were melting.

All this time, Doria had been left alone with my parents. My mother, busy saving family heirlooms, did little socializing. Dad, on the other hand, realizing he was playing host to someone who'd heard not one of his stories before, happily stepped into the breach. Doria told me later that as soon as my roommate and I had exited, my father had drawn her over to the table of maps, shown her first the territory burned by the previous fire, next the area presumed scorched this time, and then had enthusiastically launched into a lengthy account of the building of the home in which they were standing — a home, she said with an air of wonderment, he seemed to have forgotten was in danger of burning down around him.

Cracking jokes to his surgeons as he lay bleeding on a stretcher was, in other words, par.

Between the moment he was shot and the time he left surgery, Dad lost roughly half his blood volume. That he survived at all is testament to the quick reactions of Jerry Parr and his Secret Service detail and the sterling care he received once he got to George Washington University Hospital.

Those of us in the waiting room still knew few details of his condition. After what seemed an ominously long interval, we were led into the intensive care unit where Dad would be brought after surgery. He arrived attached to monitors with a breathing tube down his throat. All things considered, I thought he looked pretty good. He was certainly pale, but already alert. My mother moved gingerly to his side, telling him she loved him, reassuring him that she was there. He gazed up at her, eyes wide, unable to speak, then reached for a pad and pencil. I leaned in to see what he was writing: I CAN'T BREATHE!

Seven years a lifeguard, 77 lives saved. Now he was going to drown in his own bodily fluids while lying on a gurney in a roomful of doctors? My mother stepped back with a look of shock as the attending nurse began gently shaking her head. I glanced around at the softly beeping monitors and registered the relative calm on the faces of the medical personnel. Dad was in no immediate danger. He'd simply woken up with a tube down his throat, that, though it was keeping his lungs pumping, made him feel as though he was suffocating. I moved forward and leaned over him so that my face was directly over his. "It's okay, Dad. You're going to be okay. You've got a tube in your throat. It's like scuba diving. Just let the machine breathe for you." I have no idea why I mentioned scuba. Dad had never been diving; I had barely been diving myself. And having a plastic hose lodged in your throat is probably entirely different and quite a bit more unpleasant than breathing pressurized oxygen from a tank while communing with brightly colored fish. Nevertheless, this non sequitur seemed to calm everyone who needed calming — except, perhaps, my father, though I doubt it did him any harm.

Days later, as his recovery proceeded, I asked if he remembered my reassurances. "No." He shook his head with a slightly surprised look. "I can't say I do."

My father's recovery — a few complications notwithstanding — proceeded apace. He gained back the weight he lost. A state-of-the-art home gym was installed in the White House living quarters. Before long, Dad was boasting that he'd added an inch of muscle to his chest.

In a town where everything is rendered into political advantage (or its opposite), Dad's plucky response to near assassination earned him valuable capital during his first term. His cherished tax cuts were passed — only to be scaled back when it became apparent that trickle-down economics was, indeed, as his vice president had put it earlier, "voodoo." His approval rating in polls fell to a low of 35 percent, then revived along with economic indicators. Successive Soviet leaders were dying with distressing regularity, even as my father truculently declared Moscow's regime "the focus of evil in the modern world." A Marine barracks in Beirut, Lebanon, was bombed, killing 17

Americans and scores of others and leading to our military's withdrawal from the country. A contra insurgency funded (in part) by cocaine trafficking was battling the socialist government of Nicaragua. At home, as the economy climbed out of recession, Dad's buoyant optimism seemed to be convincing more and more potential voters that they might, after all, see America become a kind of "shining city on a hill." Before you knew it, another campaign season was coming round again.

The paradoxes inherent in Dad's character apply as well to the responses of those around him, including his family. His children might have found it passing strange that our father whom we had witnessed scampering about the house in his y-fronts, whom we knew to possess odd quirks and habits of mind, could actually have become president. Nothing unusual there — how easily can you imagine *your* father as leader of the free world? At the same time, though, from the moment he entered politics back in the sixties and people began speaking of him as presidential material, none of us ever doubted that he could win. We might disagree with him politically (two of us, anyway), but we never had second thoughts about his ability to fill the chair. This made my telling him that I didn't want him to run for reelection in 1984 a distinctly uncomfortable experience.

"You've already been shot once. That'll only give other idiots ideas — and there are plenty of them out there. I don't want to see anything like that happen again. I know you've already made up your mind, but I have to tell you, I'd prefer you didn't run."

My father, mother, and I were enjoying an early autumn afternoon on the flagstone patio behind Laurel, the president's cabin at Camp David. The trees surrounding President Dwight Eisenhower's beloved pitch and putt had long since lost their summer luster; as we sipped iced tea, a few yellow leaves drifted down. Dad had never asked his children's blessing for any of his previous political campaigns, and he wasn't soliciting mine now, but at least I was getting a heads-up before any public announcement.

Every word I spoke was true. America never lacks for rage-addled sociopaths with easy access to firearms. Who wouldn't be concerned for a loved one's safety when the nature of his job effectively paints a glowing target on his back? But I had other concerns as well, ones I couldn't share with my father.

Throughout my childhood during the sixties I had often been confused when Dad's public image diverged wildly from the reality of the fellow I saw at the dinner table most nights. He was a big softy at home, yet many people seemed to think he was a monster capable of casual cruelty. Gradually, though, as I got a bit older, I began to see that Dad, whatever success he might be enjoying in his new arena, was not at what I'd consider his personal best during this period. Outraged by college students protesting a war he never realized was a disastrous sham, flummoxed by the cultural transformation erupting on all sides (including within his own household), he became pinched and defensive. Looking at pictures from his governorship, I can see it in his face: lips compressed, left eyebrow arched, jaw tensed as if he were always choking back anger. As he aged, though, and particularly after his loss to Ford in '76, he seemed to mellow. Having served two terms as governor of California, he had already accomplished more in his life than the gang back in Dixon could ever have expected. There was more he wanted to do but little he had left to prove. Until his 1980 run, with no real responsibilities beyond the occasional speech and a weekly radio commentary, he had plenty of time to ride the trails of his beloved Rancho del Cielo. His face relaxed, taking on its familiar grandfatherly quality.

Three years into his first term as president, though, I was feeling the first shivers of concern that something beyond mellowing was affecting my father. We had always argued over this issue or that, rarely with anything approaching belligerence, but vigorously all the same. He generally had the advantage of practiced talking points backed up by staff research, but I was an unabashed, occasionally effective advocate for my own positions. "He told me you make him feel stupid," my mother once shared, to my alarm. I didn't want my father to feel stupid. If he was going to shoulder massive responsibility, I wanted him to feel on top of his game. If he was going to fulfill his duties as president, he would have to be.

Watching the first of his two debates with 1984 Democratic presidential nominee Walter Mondale, I began to experience the nausea of a bad dream coming true. At 73, Ronald Reagan would be the oldest president ever reelected. Some voters were beginning to imagine grandpa — who can never find his reading glasses — in charge of a bristling nuclear arsenal, and it was making them nervous. Worse, my father now seemed to be giving them legitimate reason for concern. My heart sank as he floundered his way through his responses, fumbling with his notes, uncharacteristically lost for words. He looked tired and bewildered.

In the debate's aftermath, as the news media turned their attention to the question of whether he was too old to serve, the spin from the White house was that he had been "overprogrammed" and "beaten up" by his advisers during debate preparations. Dad knew he'd performed badly but convinced himself he'd been "overtrained." There might have been some truth to that. D.C. is full of clever, ambitious types ever eager to prove they're the smartest wonk in the room. Lacking the benefit of wisdom, they might well have shown off at the old man's expense. My earlier worries, however, remained. Something I couldn't quite put my finger on wasn't right.

I flew out to Kansas City for the second debate two weeks later. If Dad was going to lose the election — unlikely as that still seemed — it would be because the public had gotten two consecutive doses of an out-of-touch president. This was Mondale's last shot, and, being a smart fellow, he wouldn't let it go to waste. Should Dad fall, I felt I should be there to help catch him. Like everybody close to my father, I felt protective of him. Bringing that out in people was always among his least recognized talents.

I needn't have worried. Whatever had been bothering my father, he seemed to have vanquished it, at least temporarily. Knowing he fed off the approval of crowds, his campaign staff had wisely arranged a brief appearance before an enthusiastic audience just prior to the debate. That got him properly loosened up. With a sharp slap on the behind from his younger son, he entered the debate hall that evening his usual confident self. The Mondale campaign effectively ended when Dad, responding to a question about his continued fitness for office that arrived like a slow, underhand pitch over the center of the plate, ad-libbed that he would not, "exploit, for political purposes, my opponent's youth and inexperience."

Backstage afterward, I high-fived Dad and let out a loud whoop, hoping to broadcast a mood of triumph to anyone within earshot. He had risen to the occasion. The fact that, under other circumstances and for purely political reasons, I would surely have voted for Mondale was irrelevant. This was my father; I wanted him to succeed. I'd try to change his mind about things later. He went on, of course, to one of the most dominant victories in presidential election history, leaving Mondale the winner in only his

330

home state of Minnesota.

I must admit, in the excitement of the moment that evening in Kansas City, I had failed to take much note of one of Dad's responses to a question concerning relations with the Soviet Union:

I told Mr. Gromyko [the Soviet foreign minister], we don't like their system, and they don't like ours. We're not going to change their system, and they sure better not try to change ours. But, between us, we can either destroy the world or save it. And I suggested that, certainly it was to their common interest, along with ours, to avoid a conflict and to attempt to save the world and remove the nuclear weapons.

"Save the world . . ." The Old Lifeguard had spoken, as surely as if he'd been poised on the dock at Lowell Park.

"You could have said yes."

With those words, Ronald Reagan, president of the United States, took his leave of General Secretary Mikhail Gorbachev of the Soviet Union and their negotiating site at Hofdi House in Reykjavik, Iceland, and flew back to Washington, D.C., feeling ill used and deeply disappointed. The two leaders, over the course of three riveting days, had come tantalizingly close to an agreement that would have virtually eliminated both nations' enormous nuclear stockpiles. In the end, the deal had foundered when Gorbachev's insistence that research on a strategic defense initiative (SDI) — my father's so-called Star Wars plan to build a defensive space shield — be confined to the laboratory met Dad's unwillingness to give up more robust testing.

Watching on TV as the two men parted, grim faced, in the rain and gloom, I tried not to blame myself.

Several years earlier, prior to my father's announcement of SDI, I had spoken with him about the possibility of some sort of umbrella defense against nuclear attack. Dad's greatest horror as president — and one hopes he's not alone in this — was the thought that through misunderstanding, unforeseen circumstance, or some bizarre technical glitch, he would be compelled to launch our nuclear missiles on warning. "I have to believe the Russian people are no different from Americans," he would tell me. "Hell, they're victims of their own government. Why should millions of them have to die, along with millions of our people, because leaders on both sides couldn't work things out?" Having no technical expertise whatsoever, I nevertheless broached the topic with him of developing some kind of barrier that would render thermonuclear warheads ineffective and, therefore, obsolete. It's not like it wasn't a reasonable question. We were pouring trillions of tax dollars into our defense apparatus; why couldn't the Pentagon team up with NASA and MIT to produce a system of satellites capable of unleashing a solar-powered electromagnetic pulse that would turn incoming warheads into recyclable waste? Granted, it was the sort of question you might pose after a couple of bong hits in your dorm room, but still — Dad wasn't the only one who wanted to save the planet. There was a long silence on the other end of the phone. "Well . . ."

We were not speaking over a secure line. He couldn't divulge in any detail the plans I later realized were already being hatched. The edge of excitement in his voice, though, told me I'd struck a nerve. He allowed that he had been thinking along similar lines before enthusiastically reciting his mantra about the shared humanity of Russians and Americans. Dad never imagined defeating the Soviet Union militarily. He understood very well the concept of mutually assured destruction and didn't much like it. He knew, too, that the Soviet economy was on the brink of collapse. Matching our military spending to begin with was killing them; being forced to counter SDI might just push them over the edge. His hope was to encourage the inevitable demise of the Soviet Union — freeing millions from an oppressive totalitarian regime and ending the Cold War — all without having to fire a shot. He didn't lack for doubters.

I didn't really imagine that my unwitting encouragement of SDI had led to the collapse of the most concerted effort to scale back nuclear arsenals since the Cold War began. Still, having since come to the realization that the idea of shooting missiles out of the sky with other missiles only made sense as a cash cow for the military-industrial-congressional complex (President Eisenhower's original formulation of the phrase made famous in his farewell speech), I was unhappy that Star Wars had caused such seemingly fruitful talks to end on a sour note. It was certainly a letdown from the two men's previous meeting in Geneva, Switzerland.

On Tuesday, November 19, 1985, I found myself inside the château Fleur d'Eau, awaiting the start of the first U.S.-Soviet summit since 1979. George Shultz, Paul Nitze, and the entire heavyweight squad were on hand. In town to cover the scene for *Playboy* magazine, I had wangled my way into the château with the understanding that anything I saw or heard there would be off the record. I was just an invited fly on the wall. The last thing I expected was to get into a stare down with General Secretary Gorbachev.

Gorbachev had disembarked his armored ZIL limousine in homburg and overcoat moments earlier, to be greeted by a hatless, coatless, and much taller Ronald Reagan advancing down the château steps toward him. How had he perceived my father in that moment? "Sunshine and clear sky," as he told Dad's biographer, Edmund Morris, years later.

It may have had something to do with my being the only person within several kilometers wearing blue jeans, or maybe it was my red flannel shirt, but as Dad and Gorbachev seated themselves in front of a picturesque fire for the obligatory photo op, the general secretary gave me a rather disapproving once over. Before I fully realized what was happening, we had locked eyes.

Many seasons had passed since I was the fifth-grade stare down runner-up; I feared I might now be overmatched. Gorbachev possesses a formidable mind, and I could feel the power of it behind his eyes. While frankly enjoying the absurdity of the moment — seriously, did he, at least, not have better things to be focusing on? — I couldn't help feeling, as the seconds ticked past, as though I were waging this impromptu contest on behalf of my fellow Americans. How long could Gorbachev possibly hang on with flashbulbs going off in his face and Sam Donaldson squawking in the background? After what seemed an interminable stretch of time, he wavered ever so slightly, then crumbled, and, with a final, slightly contemptuous look, turned back to the more mundane pursuits of national survival and world peace.

Later, from a familiar position outside a door left ajar, I listened as Dad, in the opening plenary session, ran through a long litany of complaints about Soviet misbehavior around the world. When he finished, Gorbachev responded with exasperation — but also, I thought, with a chuckle in his voice that held promise — that you couldn't seriously ascribe every unpleasantness on earth to Soviet meddling.

As this back-and-forth was going on, several uniformed Russian personnel on the other side of the room regarded me and a couple of other Americans who had joined me at the door with displeasure, upset at our eavesdropping. I was too intent to pay them much mind, as I was listening for something in particular. When I heard it, I turned to our Russian friends and mimed with waggling fingers two people walking: Dad had chosen his moment to invite Gorbachev for a private chat in a small guesthouse a short stroll away. This companionable interlude had been planned in advance by the American team, and the guesthouse had been duly prepared with a roaring fire to set the proper mood. My father counted on his being irresistible in one-on-one encounters, which was more or less true most of the time. But would his boyish Dixon spirit work its peculiar magic on such a man as the general secretary, one whose world was colored in far starker tones?

Their conversation was scheduled to last no more than 10 minutes — just long enough for Ronald Reagan's high beams to penetrate the Slavic gloom, his advisers undoubtedly thought, but not so long that he might fall prey to Communist trickery and give away the store.

An hour later a small knot of thoroughly amazed onlookers was still standing outside the guesthouse, discreetly beyond the sight lines of the two leaders, as they continued to talk. Now and again, one of us would lean forward to catch a glimpse of polished shoe leather or tailored shoulder and reassure everyone that, yes, the Russian and the American were still at it. When Dad and Gorbachev finally emerged from their fireside bonding session, no grand bargains had been reached, but a swelling sense of optimism seemed to be pushing back against the Geneva gray. War between the world's two superpowers was somehow suddenly less thinkable.

Had all that been undone by my father's intransigence at Reykjavik? Or by Gorbachev's trap, sprung at the last possible moment, intended to cripple SDI and buy himself and his beleaguered system some time? Dad, fuming in the backseat of his car to chief of staff Donald Regan all the way to Keflavik Airport, may have feared so — though there's no doubt whom he blamed: Brezhnev, Chernenko, Andropov, all of these general secretaries had died during Dad's tenure, before any useful rapprochement could get under way. Now this younger, more promising Russian leader arises, and together they come within a whisker of realizing Dad's cherished dream of a world rid of nuclear weapons, only to see an agreement collapse over his other dream, an impermeable defensive space shield. Such opportunities don't arise often and, with the clock ticking on his final term in office, Dad knew time was running out. The mood in his limo was deeply gloomy.

Gorbachev, speaking with Prime Minister Steingrimur Hermannsson of Iceland on the airport tarmac a short while later, proved more optimistic and more prescient. "This," Gorbachev told Hermannsson, huddling beneath a shared umbrella against blowing sleet, "is the beginning of the end of the Cold War." He was correct. The "failure" at Reykjavik led, the following year, to the Intermediate-range Nuclear Forces Treaty (INF), eliminating a whole class of nuclear weapons. INF led, in turn, to the strategic arms reduction treaties (START I and II) in 1991 and 1993. Neither man could have anticipated, though, that only five years later, the end of the end would come, and the Soviet Union would cease to exist.

From the White House "Daily Diary of President Ronald Reagan," February 28, 1987, 7:30 P.M.: "The President had dinner with: The First Lady; Ronald P. Reagan, son."

This bland entry in the log of comings and goings, calls and visitors to the president's house fails to adequately capture one of the most uncomfortable moments of my life. I had visited the White House before, to be sure. Doria and I had spent a couple of Christmas holidays there and had slept over after attending inaugurals and State of the Union addresses. We both had had enough experience to prefer the Queens' Bedroom, with its firmer mattress, to the more celebrated Lincoln Bedroom across the hall, which (according to my sister Maureen) harbored its own tall, gaunt, and reddish-hued apparition. However, I had never paid a call with anything on my mind beyond filial obligation. This visit was different.

Dad's powers of denial are justifiably legend. He could turn an obscene insult into a heartfelt expression of support — literally. Sitting in the back of the presidential limo, returning from some event or another, Doria and I watched it happen. Around this time Dad had gotten it into his head to revive the thumbs-up gesture. Traveling the country, he'd waggle an optimistic thumb to one and all — no hand sign has ever suited a man so well. As we drove past a crowd of onlookers on this day, however, we encountered a fellow promoting another gesture, one requiring the flourish of an entirely different digit. Somehow he had managed to duck under the police barrier and was eager to get up close and personal. His stiff middle finger loomed large, thrusting itself toward the sunny countenance of the president, smiling behind bulletproof glass no more than an arm's length away. If memory serves, the term "motherfucker" may also have been snarlingly deployed. Dad took all this in and, without missing a beat, turned to the rest of us with his own squared-off thumb held triumphantly aloft and said, "You see, I think it's catching on!"

It isn't ordinarily in my nature to be cruel, but some things do need to be faced squarely. I had been watching as revelations of arms being shipped to Iran in hopes of securing the release of hostages held in Lebanon had unfolded. The basic outlines of this unfortunate gambit were now unpleasantly apparent, yet my father, in public statements, seemed woefully behind the curve, if not out of the loop altogether. He needed to own up to what he'd obviously approved (arms for hostages) and to make it clear that those who took part in the other part of the scheme (funds to the contras) would be prosecuted. I had come to the conclusion that a little tough love from his youngest might encourage him in the right direction.

It wouldn't be the first time he'd been warned by his children about nefarious characters associated with his National Security

Council. Some months before Maureen had called me, concerned about rogue elements within the NSC who felt entitled to pursue their own agendas, our father be damned. Feeling that my imprimatur would gain her a more timely audience, she asked me to set up a meeting with Dad when he was next on the West Coast. Though she delivered no specific warning that morning about a scheme to get the Israelis to sell American arms to the Iranians so monies could be diverted to the contras in Nicaragua, the thrust of Maureen's argument — there were people at the NSC doing their own thing without bothering to inform you — was crystal clear. Dad heard my sister out, but I could tell he was disinclined to credit her information. We, his children, were not experts. We did not have access to all the information available to him. We could be troublesome and argumentative. If anything was really wrong, surely "the fellas" would have let him know. Besides, this revelation of corruption within the ranks was just not something he wanted to hear under any circumstances. Dad, ever guileless and straightforward, never quite grasped, for instance, that the seemingly respectful, decorated soldier fairly beaming with flattery, who had, on rare occasions, been brought to meet him in the Oval Office, had in fact conspired with his national security adviser, among others, to violate the law.

Virtually all the details of this perfidy had been exposed by the time I sat down to dinner with my father and mother beneath the nineteenth-century murals on the family dining room's curving walls, more than enough to suggest that this was the sort of affair that risked tarnishing an entire presidency. I expected, upon arriving at the White House, to find a chief executive fully immersed in the details of the scandal, busily formulating a response, and grimly determined to send a few heads rolling. Instead, I found my father lost in a fog of depression and denial. Though he had received the Tower Report a couple of days before, which described the illicit arms transfers, he was still reciting talking points that now lagged a week behind the news cycle.

I couldn't tell if anything I said that night sank in. With my mother sitting by in silent assent, I acted both the good and bad cop roles, ranging from reasonable and sympathetic to shocked and affronted. Looking back, I've often wondered if I was too harsh.

Years later, when his diaries were published, I was relieved to see what he had written after our rocky evening: "Ron arrived. He came from the coast to plead with me — out of his love for me — to take forceful action & charge of the situation. I was deeply touched."

I, for my part, was deeply concerned, my old worries back with a vengeance. Wanting to get a look at my father during the course of his day, I asked if I could tag along with him the following Monday.

From Dad's diary, March 2: "Ron asked if he could spend a day in my office to see what my job was like. So I said yes & he was in all of the meetings etc."

Not quite all the meetings, as I recall. A CIA brief would have required a clearance level not even presidential offspring are easily granted; according to the White House log, I stepped out of the Oval Office for four minutes during the afternoon while Acting Director Robert Gates held forth. Otherwise, I was along for the whole ride.

It was Howard Baker's first day as chief of staff, replacing Donald Regan, whose tenure had come to a bitter end when he made the fatal mistake of hanging up on his boss's wife not once, but twice. Howard was accompanied into the Oval Office for his first official meeting as chief by Vice President Bush. Sitting around the Resolute desk — built from the timbers of a British arctic exploration vessel sent to search for the doomed party of explorer Sir John Franklin and given to President Rutherford B. Hayes in 1880 by Queen Victoria — we welcomed Howard. Then the three men discussed candidates for CIA director, and the elder Bush made fun of my suit, wondering whether I'd purchased it at Hialeah race track. I inquired in turn whether he'd copped his from a dead banker he found laying in the street — White House meets frat house. My father was pleased that Howard was onboard. He was well respected in Washington. He was smart. He was a grown-up. Plus, he was an amiable, easygoing sort, which would be a relief after the prickly Regan. Howard was happy, because the new gig gave him a graceful way out of the upcoming presidential contest. He didn't want to run, but his stature would otherwise oblige him to make the effort. Bush, for his part, seemed satisfied to have needled me about my colorful tweed.

A cabinet meeting, an issues briefing lunch, a soporific meeting with Republican mayors — the day wore on. Dad seemed most animated when his longtime pollster, Richard Wirthlin, dropped by to share the latest numbers and informed him that a majority of respondents didn't feel their president was telling the truth about the arms shipments to Iran. Dad didn't much care about his approval rating dropping to 44 percent, but the thought that he was perceived a liar stung. By 2:45, however, the day was more or less over. Dad hung around the Oval for another hour and 10 minutes, making three phone calls to politicians he knew well. I noticed that during the calls, the longest of which lasted 5 minutes, that he was relying on scripted cards. At 3:55, it was back to the living quarters.

Maureen was in town that Monday evening, and, while my mother attended a Just Say No event, we had dinner with our father. He would be giving a speech that Wednesday, acknowledging that the "initiative" to Iran had gone badly awry. I was pleased to see that since my arrival he had begun to wrap his mind, however grudgingly, around the full dimensions of the issue. He was still depressed and listless, though, and I was still worried.

I don't want to give the impression, when I recall my concerns about him, that my father was catatonic or mumbling incoherently during this or any period. Having known him all my life, I was no doubt especially attuned to any changes in his demeanor or hitch in his cognition. He was, at the time of my visit, a 76-year-old man who had survived a near fatal shooting and surgery for colon cancer. As old men will, he had learned to conserve his energy for crucial moments. The Iran-contra affair — its shady characters with murky motives, its architecture of internal betrayal — was a perfect example of the sort of mess Dad was ill suited, at any age, in any condition, to anticipate, head off, or reckon with once it blew up in his face. Yet, little more than three months later, he would stand at the Brandenburg Gate in Berlin, the dividing barrier between East and West, and, in one of the defining moments of the Cold War, challenge his old negotiating partner, Mikhail Gorbachev, to "tear down this wall." It was a phrase that neither his new chief of staff nor his national security adviser, Colin Powell, wanted him to employ. He showed better judgment in overruling them. And we all know what happened to the Berlin Wall. Dad could clearly still get up for the big moments.

I could not shake my feeling, though, that something was amiss.

Before leaving office he would endure one more brush with a fact that, no matter how he might try, could not be edited from his script: his wife's diagnosis of breast cancer and subsequent mastectomy. The awful reality of the situation caught up with him as he waited for her to return from surgery at Bethesda Naval Hospital. Sitting by himself in a sterile hospital room, he was, at last, no longer a world leader but a frightened and lonely man. His White House physician, John Hutton, worried about him, but knowing Dad would be reluctant to seek comfort from another man, asked a nurse, Paula Trivette, to check on him. In her arms he broke down, sobbing uncontrollably. That he could do nothing, in this instance, to spare his Nancy from suffering was more than he could bear.

In July 1989, barely six months out of office, my father visited friends in Mexico. While out riding he was thrown when his horse shied at something in the trailside scrub. That my father, even at age 78, would be bucked off his mount was, in itself, an ominous sign. It's a wonder he didn't break any bones, but he did hit his head hard enough to cause a sizable contusion. After initially refusing medical attention, he ultimately relented and was transported to a hospital in San Diego. Surgeons opening his skull to relieve pressure on the brain emerged from the operating room with the news that they had detected what they took to be probable signs of Alzheimer's disease. No formal diagnosis was given, as far as I know. I have since learned from a doctor who happened to be interning at the hospital when my father was brought in that surgeons involved in his care, in what my informant characterized as "shameful" behavior, violated my father's right to medical privacy by subsequently gossiping about his condition.

Doctors recommended to my mother that further tests of cognition be conducted the following year to measure any decline. Those tests, at the Mayo Clinic, confirmed the initial suspicion of Alzheimer's.

I've seen no evidence that my father (or anyone else) was aware of his medical condition while he was in office. Had the diagnosis been made in, say, 1987, would he have stepped down? I believe he would have. Far less was known about the disease then, of course, than is known now. Today we are aware that the physiological and neurological changes associated with Alzheimer's can be in evidence years, even decades, before identifiable symptoms arise. The question, then, of whether my father suffered from the beginning stages of Alzheimer's while in office more or less answers itself.

Does this delegitimize his presidency? Only to the extent that President Kennedy's Addison's disease or Lincoln's clinical depression undermine theirs. Better, it seems to me, to judge our presidents by what they actually accomplish than what hidden factors may be weighing on them. We are entitled to approve or disapprove of my father's conduct in office irrespective of his medical condition. That likely condition, though, serves as a reminder that when we elect presidents, we elect human beings with all their foibles and weaknesses, psychological and physiological.

While I would not want to overstate this case, I find something courageous (albeit unknowingly so) in my father's dedicated pursuit — even in the face of his declining powers — of peaceful rapprochement with the world's other nuclear superpower. He never stopped wanting to save the world.

My father might himself have suspected that all was not as it should be. As far back as August 1986 he had been alarmed to discover, while flying over the familiar canyons north of Los Angeles, that he could no longer summon their names.

Had he been diagnosed while in office, there would have been no question about the ethics of informing him immediately — he would have had to be told. Once he was back in private life, however, the circumstances were entirely different. My mother made the difficult, but in retrospect, I believe, wise

350

and kind decision to put off telling him until it could no longer be avoided. Knowing her husband as she did, she correctly intuited that such a diagnosis — a terminal illness with no hope of cure — once acknowledged might send him spiraling into a deep depression, jeopardizing any chance he had for a few relatively good years before impenetrable darkness descended.

By November 1994 that sorry duty had become a necessity. His decline had become obvious even to a casual observer. Media outlets were beginning to prepare stories that would reveal his condition. So on November 5 of that year, having been informed of his prognosis, Dad sat down and wrote what amounted to his farewell letter to the American public. It is, in its way, a beautiful document that speaks volumes about its author. Dad's mental capacity may have been diminished, but his character remained intact. I could summarize the letter, but I'd rather let my father speak for himself:

My Fellow Americans,
    I have recently been told that I am one of the millions of Americans who will be afflicted with Alzheimer's disease.
    Upon learning this news, Nancy and I had to decide whether as private citizens

we would keep this a private matter or whether we would make this news known in a public way. In the past, Nancy suffered from breast cancer and I had my cancer surgeries. We found through our open disclosures we were able to raise public awareness. We were happy that as a result, many more people underwent testing. They were treated in early stages and able to return to normal, healthy lives.

So now, we feel it is important to share it with you. In opening our hearts, we hope this might promote a greater awareness of this condition. Perhaps it will encourage a clearer understanding of the individuals and families who are afflicted by it.

At the moment I feel just fine. I intend to live the remainder of the years God gives me on this earth doing the things I have always done. I will continue to share life's journey with my beloved Nancy and my family. I plan to enjoy the great outdoors and stay in touch with my friends and supporters.

Unfortunately, as Alzheimer's disease progresses, the family often bears a heavy burden. I only wish there was some way I could spare Nancy from this painful experience. When the time comes I am confident that with your help she will face it with faith and courage.

In closing let me thank you, the American people, for giving me the great honor of allowing me to serve as your president. When the Lord calls me home, whenever that may be, I will leave with the greatest love for this country of ours and eternal optimism for its future.

I now begin the journey that will lead me to the sunset of my life. I know that for America there will always be a bright dawn ahead.

Thank you my friends. May God always bless you.

Sincerely,
Ronald Reagan

I can only hope that, under similar circumstances, I would be able to muster the grace and courage to pen a similar letter.

It should come as no surprise when victims of Alzheimer's, whose minds are being ravaged in unpredictable ways, exhibit bizarre behavior, even becoming verbally abusive or violent. Far more often than not, this is the disease talking and not the revelation of an underlying flaw in character. More unusual is the patient who, throughout the course of the illness, retains unaltered his natural disposition. Predictably enough, that was how my father decided to play it.

After signing off his final letter to the public, Dad seemed to relinquish himself to the disease: no more speeches to give, no more public obligations to be met, the roar of the crowd a fading memory and with it that energizing infusion of attention and approval that buoyed his step across the world's stage.

Tragically, among his private pleasures, riding was one of the earliest to go. John Barletta, his Secret Service agent and longtime equestrian partner, wept when he had to tell Dad he could no longer be trusted on the back of a horse. "I know, John," said Dad, comforting him with a hand on the shoulder. "It's all right."

For a time he continued going to his office in Century City, a few minutes from his home. He seemed, as always, to appreciate the routine. Visiting from Seattle, I would find him at his desk, fingering a copy of the day's schedule that existed only to give him something reassuring to hold. We would sit for a while, mostly quiet; ironically, for a man dubbed "the Great Communicator," facility with language was among the first of his faculties to desert him. He would nibble at the chocolate truffles I'd brought with an air of deep concentration. Now and then,

I'd gently try to lead him toward whatever memories might be available. Eventually, he no longer recognized me.

When the office became untenable, he retreated homeward. Swimming retained its appeal for a time, though it was painful to see the once masterful lifeguard propped up in the shallow end by a nurse and security agent, reduced to the indignity of water wings. During one phase Dad saw it as his special mission to keep their small pool free of the magnolia leaves that would blow down from an overhanging tree. His agents, sweetly patient, would keep enough windfall on hand to ensure a steady supply for him to pluck from the water.

When he could no longer amble down to the pool, when outdoors in general had lost its fascination, he headquartered in the den, watching TV and fitfully napping. Finally, when walking anywhere or even standing upright became too perilous — and when my mother, desperately fatigued, made the wrenching decision that they must, for the first time in over 50 years of marriage, sleep separately — he took to a state-of-the-art hospital bed wheeled into what had once been his home office. Here, in his last months, he would hold court, uncomplaining and gently agreeable, a silent pasha whose benign presence filled the room. Here, he would end his days.

His nurse, a devoted Irishwoman whose soft brogue I liked to imagine was especially comforting to Dad, called us to his side with a nod and a look the meaning of which we all understood.

Shifting over, the nurse made room for my mother, who took her place near my father's head, stroking his hair and petting his shoulder. Next to her, Patti held his left hand. I stood over Patti's shoulder, my hand on his left knee. There was no reason to expect anything other than a peaceful, uneventful cessation of life. Dad had lain mostly unmoving for weeks, barely opening his eyes. His breathing had now become faint, the interval between inhalations growing steadily longer. We murmured words of love and affection and waited, unaware that Dad had in store one last surprise.

Just as it seemed the breath was about to leave his body for good, he opened his eyes. I do not mean to say they merely fluttered or took on a fixed stare. No, there was both intensity and intention behind them, eyes that all at once appeared vividly blue, bluer by far than the twilight hazel in my memory. He lifted his head from his pillow, turning and straining toward the sound of his wife's voice. In his gaze was a fierceness that seemed to reflect the desperate exertion necessary for this final expenditure of life force. Early in my parents' marriage, my father had told his bride she was the first thing he wanted to see upon waking each morning and the last thing he ever wanted to see. Now, in the critical moment, calling on some deep reservoir of strength hidden away in his ravaged mind, he was somehow willing himself to fulfill that desire.

His eyes found the face of the woman who, for more than half a century, had formed the core of his private world. "I love you, honey. I love you" was all she could say — was all she needed to say. Sometimes eternity is compressed into an instant, the celestial wheel seems to catch and hold — but only for an instant. The blue flame guttered and extinguished. His eyes dimmed. With a quiet exhalation, my father settled back onto his pillow and died.

The doctor looked down at his watch and then to the nurse. "Time of death: 1:00 P.M." "One P.M.," she nodded.

Ninety-three years and then some since a February blizzard blew over the plains of northern Illinois, leaving the air clear and the black sky hung with frozen diamonds above a sleeping town, Tampico, buried in drifts. What is that sound echoing across the untracked snow in the hour before first light? Who is that newborn crying? On the east side of Main Street, above the bakery, a single window is illuminated. There, a story begins. Here, in a hillside home beneath Los Angeles's buttermilk haze, it ends.

The peerless lifeguard of Lowell Park; Eureka College's finest swimmer and most dedicated gridiron fanatic; undaunted diver of the Hennepin Canal; intrepid wanderer of field and wood; solitary spinner of daydreams from attic relics; spreader of Dixon spirit and lifelong seeker of a mythic shining city; Dutch to his father; Dad to his kids; Ronnie to his wife and friends; but forever his mother's "perfectly wonderful" Ronald: The storyteller has gone home.

His story, though, lives on.

EPILOGUE:
NEVER-ENDING STORY

One hundred years after my father's birth, what accounts for his uncanny magic? He has been gone from public life for nearly 20 years, dead for over half a decade, yet he seems to have remained peculiarly and vividly alive in the minds of many Americans. On the left, he is routinely lambasted for everything from the scourge of Reaganomics to the country's militarism (though Barack Obama, bipartisan hand perennially outstretched, has genuflected in his direction). On the right, he remains an object of almost fetishistic veneration. GOP candidates strenuously compete to see who can invoke his name in the most reverential way

Predictably, much of the attention showered on Dad these days, positive and negative, misses the mark. While it's true that many unfortunate political tendencies metastasized during the eighties — kowtowing to religious extremists, denigrating and ignoring empirical science, stoking irrational grassroots fears while cynically pandering to moneyed interests — they cannot all be attributed to Ronald Reagan. Those tendencies long predate him and became far more extreme after he left the scene. Beyond a fondness for nonintrusive government and lower taxes (you'll recall that the top marginal tax rate for most of his years in office was 50 percent), he had little in common with the rage mongering infecting his party today. Short-circuiting the functions of government, potentially driving the country into ruin just to score political points by pinning the blame on the opposition, are tactics he would consider unpatriotic, not to mention undemocratic.

Of course, I don't want to make the same mistake that others have in speaking on behalf of my father. The world has changed since he left office. I can't know with certainty — and neither can anyone else — how he would have reacted to developments he couldn't have anticipated during his presidency. Many of those who presume to speak in his voice scarcely met him, if at all. None truly knew him. Dad and I, on the other hand, were well acquainted.

Understandably, most people, whatever their

political beliefs, relate to my father as president of the United States. For eight years, he was my president, too. He was my father, though, for my entire life and nearly half of his. You remember, perhaps, signal events like his inauguration, the summit meetings, his words following the *Challenger* disaster. My memories of my father start with his lifting me over his head and "flying" me through the rooms of our house, dipping under doorways, banking left and right, mimicking the drone of a propeller engine, before gently swooping me into bed for the night. There, using one of his early nicknames for me, he would sing me a little song in his soft, unself-conscious tenor:

Old Skipper Reagan was a merry old soul
And he went to Heaven on a telegraph pole.
But the pole was thin and Skipper fell in,
Right in heaven up to his chin.

In my hands is a note from one of my father's nurses, written on a pad embossed OFFICE OF RONALD REAGAN. It is dated April 25, 2000, "about 1:00 PM." My mother gave it to me some years ago, hoping, I think, to reassure me that even as the end neared, Dad still cared for his children. It recalls one of his increasingly brief flurries of focused mental activity while descending into the throes of late-stage Alzheimer's:

> 3 mentions of Ron in about a 20 min. span of time.

Like all my siblings, I loved my father deeply, at times longingly. He was easy to love but hard to know. He was seldom far from our minds, but you couldn't help wondering sometimes whether he remembered you once you were out of his sight.

Something in his innocent optimism, his guileless wonder at the world, made you want to shield him from harsh reality. His dreams might strike you as unlikely and naïve, but the way he cherished them made you reluctant to shatter his illusions, loath to inflict such pain. And who wouldn't, after all, want to live in a shining city?

At its heart, this is a story of fathers and sons: Old Thomas O'Regan, bog Irish peasant, and his soap-maker-turned-farmer son, Michael, who brought the family to America; Jack and Dutch; my father and I. We all grow up idolizing, dethroning, and, with luck, later befriending our fathers, but can we really know them? Do they care to know us? Is there an older chapter in the human saga?

At his own father's funeral, Dad was overcome by a wave of despair until, he said, he heard Jack's voice telling him, "I'm okay." I have not, as of yet, heard my father's voice whispering in my ear, but I haven't stopped listening.

Venturing into the corners of his early life, peering into the attic sunbeams of his boyhood, walking the shoreline of his riverside domain, I have done my best to find my father. I will not pretend that I have done so with any great success. The human mind is unfathomable; even our loved ones retain their mystery. My father, especially, held his secrets close — even, at times, from his beloved wife. I believe I have caught glimpses of him, though — in a quiet corner among artifacts seductively strange, imagination whirling, or on his lifeguard chair, keeping the planets in their proper orbits so that he might dream his dreams in tranquility. He was the solitary storyteller whose great opus, religiously tended always, was his own self.

In the end, the joy of my journey — visiting Dad's former haunts, discovering unknown family members, teasing forth the threads of his personality — was in the seeking. Now, holding this creased, dog-eared scrap of paper from over a decade ago, I feel my eyes start to sting; the words swim across the page. Yet there is a reassuring satisfaction as well in discovering a moment, however fleeting, when my father was searching for me.

ABOUT THE AUTHOR

Ron Reagan is the son of President Ronald Reagan and First Lady Nancy Reagan. Formerly a dancer with the Joffrey Ballet, he has been a political commentator and cohost of MSNBC's *Connected: Coast to Coast,* as well as host of *The Ron Reagan Show* on Air America Radio. He has written for numerous magazines, including *Newsweek, Playboy, Esquire,* and *The New Yorker.* He lives in Seattle with his wife, Doria.

The employees of Thorndike Press hope you have enjoyed this Large Print book. All our Thorndike, Wheeler, and Kennebec Large Print titles are designed for easy reading, and all our books are made to last. Other Thorndike Press Large Print books are available at your library, through selected bookstores, or directly from us.

For information about titles, please call:
(800) 223-1244

or visit our Web site at:
http://gale.cengage.com/thorndike

To share your comments, please write:
Publisher
Thorndike Press
295 Kennedy Memorial Drive
Waterville, ME 04901